James Tissot

James Tissot

VICTORIAN LIFE / MODERN LOVE

Nancy Rose Marshall and Malcolm Warner

The American Federation of Arts · Yale Center for British Art

Yale University Press · New Haven & London

ISBN 0-300-08173-1 (clothbound)
ISBN 0-939606-89-2 (paperback)
Library of Congress Catalog Card Number 99-62074

PHOTOGRAPHIC CREDITS
Images are supplied by the owners of the works and
are reproduced by their permission, with the following
additional credits. Richard Caspole: figs. 1, 2, 7, 12, 15, 16, 17,
19, 21, 22, 26, 28, 29, 30, 31; Michael Tropea: nos. 5, 6, 11–13,
21, 22, 24, 26, 29–36, 38, 41, 42, 48–51, 53, 56, 58, 59, 61–64,
69–75; John Parnell: nos. 88–93; Arturo Piera: no. 1; RMN-
Jean Schormans: no. 7; RMN-Hervé Lewandowski: no. 8;
Christies' Images Ltd. 1999: fig. 5.

Front cover, no. 44 (detail); back cover, no. 43;
frontispiece, no. 27 (detail); details of the following
works appear on the pages indicated: p. 8, no. 20;
p. 10, no. 10; p. 17, no. 23; p. 20, no. 66; p. 22, no. 1;
p. 34, no. 8; p. 50, no. 15; p. 60, no. 18; p. 104, no. 45;
p. 120, no. 52; p. 146, no. 67; p. 162, no. 87

Design and composition by Julie Lavorgna
Printed in Singapore

PUBLISHED ON THE OCCASION OF A TRAVELING EXHIBITION

Yale Center for British Art, New Haven, Connecticut
September 22 – November 28, 1999

Musée du Québec, Canada
December 15, 1999 – March 12, 2000

Albright-Knox Art Gallery, Buffalo, New York
March 24 – July 2, 2000

The exhibition is supported by an indemnity from the
Federal Council on the Arts and the Humanities

NOTE ON THE PRINTS. Unless otherwise
indicated, the prints are from the published
editions and the dimensions given are those
of the plate. The abbreviation "W." followed
by a number refers to Michael Wentworth's
catalogue raisonné of 1978 (see *Bibliography*).

Contents

Foreword

James Tissot remains one of the most attractive and fascinating figures in Anglo-French art of the late nineteenth century. A Frenchman who adopted an English spelling of his first name and who painted his most characteristic works at the zenith of Victorian England, Tissot deserves and repays the close scrutiny of a one-man exhibition. Yet it is over thirty years since the last American retrospective. Much has happened to our knowledge of Tissot during that time, thanks to the scholarship of Michael Wentworth and Willard Misfeldt and to the research of the joint curators of this exhibition, Malcolm Warner, Senior Curator of Paintings and Sculpture at the Yale Center for British Art, and Nancy Rose Marshall, who recently completed her doctoral dissertation on the artist. Dr. Marshall has brought both fresh insights and the most recent findings of Tissot scholarship to her entries in the catalogue.

The charm and glamour of Tissot's art have been readily acknowledged, as have the stylishness and wit of the paintings. What Malcolm Warner has brought out in the selection of works and in his introductory essay is a deeper and more penetrating analysis of Tissot's ambiguities and ironies. The foibles of love and defeats of passion, the shifting relationship between men and women in a rich, materialistic society, the self-interest of the leisured classes—these and other themes are the potent suggestions of the exhibition. Set in the luxury and comfort of upper-middle- to upper-class Victorian life, Tissot's paintings and prints nonetheless look forward to the complexities of modern love.

In every way Tissot fulfilled the program of Baudelaire, Manet, and the Impressionists to be a "painter of modern life." Yet he refused the Impressionists' invitation to show with them. He kept his distance, and his reputation has suffered a little as a result. This exhibition, we hope, will play a key part in restoring Tissot to his deserved place as one of the best observers and most brilliant recorders of the pains and passions of life in the modern age.

An exhibition of this complexity accrues many debts. We wish to thank the lenders, both individual and institutional, who have parted so generously with their Tissots. In particular we want to acknowledge the assistance of the Illinois collector who has supported the exhibition from its inception and lent from his magnificent holdings of Tissot's prints.

We are delighted to be working with two such distinguished institutions as the Albright-Knox Art Gallery in Buffalo and the Musée du Québec.

The staffs of both the American Federation of Arts and the Yale Center for British art have played a keen and critical role in guaranteeing the success of the exhibition and catalogue alike. In particular we want to acknowledge AFA staff members Thomas Padon, director of exhibitions; Klaus Ottmann, curator of exhibitions; Robin Kaye Goodman, exhibitions assistant; Karen Convertino, registrar; Katey Brown, head of education; Brian Boucher, assistant curator of education; and Lisbeth Mark, director of communications; and Yale Center staff members Beth Miller, assistant director for development; Senja Foster, public relations manager; Linda Friedlaender, curator of education; and Julie Lavorgna, coordinator of publications.

Lastly, we wish to thank the Benefactors Circle of the AFA for their generous support of the exhibition.

Serena Rattazzi
Director
American Federation of Arts

Patrick McCaughey
Director
Yale Center for British Art

The Painter of Modern Love

Malcolm Warner

At the heart of James Tissot's work as an artist lies the idea of the modern, the appearance and character of the present as they distinguish it from the past. Like his friends Edgar Degas, Edouard Manet, and James McNeill Whistler, he learned much from Charles Baudelaire's brilliant essay on the aesthetics of modernity, *Le Peintre de la vie moderne*, published in 1863. Baudelaire called upon artists to treat contemporary life in all its mundane details as seriously as the historical, biblical, mythic, and allegorical subjects of traditional high art. The "painter of modern life" whom Baudelaire took as his model was a quite different kind of artist, the minor draughtsman Constantin Guys. But some of his chapters on aspects of modernity, "Beauty, Fashion, and Happiness," "Manners and Modes," "The Annals of War," "The Dandy," "Women: Honest Ones, and Others," read like a prescription for Tissot's themes and interests.[1] Above all, Tissot deals with the manners and customs of modern love: the drama of attraction and flirtation, body language and eye contact, the signs of availability, the many degrees of prostitution, the workings of passion, its frustrations, rivalries and cross purposes, the sorrows of separation and loss—all of these in the particular forms they took in Paris and London in the later nineteenth century.

He was nothing if not his own man. In his character and his art he tended toward a stylish individualism, even contrariness, and his taste for the unexpected was apparent from the outset. He began his career as an eccentric type of *anti-modernist*. The artist hero of his youth, a wildly offbeat enthusiasm for a student in Paris, was the Belgian painter Hendrik Leys. Leys painted to an all-over, high degree of finish, leaving no rough brushwork, which was a quality Tissot always admired. But in that respect he differed little from Tissot's official teachers in Paris, Louis Lamothe and Hippolyte Flandrin. The real attraction was his subject matter: Leys's specialty was faithfully reconstructed scenes set in the sixteenth century in northern Europe. Tissot had spent most of his childhood in northern towns full of medieval

architecture, and the Belgian painter's ability to bring the past to life in the kind of place he knew well was far more exciting than the classical and biblical subjects favored by his teachers. His early, Leysian *Marguerite à l'église* (no. 2), a narrative of seduction and remorse, not only announces his lifelong interest in the complications of love; it also shows the sumptuous materialism that runs through all his work, as well as hinting at the religiosity that was to mark the final phase of his career.

He moved into the modern-life subject in the mid 1860s. To put it another way, he stayed with the historical approach he had taken in his Leysian pictures, focusing on those things particular to a period, merely changing the period to the present. He took up the challenge of modernity later and more cautiously than his avant-garde friends, looking for a new artistic direction partly because his pictures were criticized for being too much like Leys. But the move could hardly have been more successful. He began to attract more favorable reviews, became highly sought-after by patrons and collectors, and was soon able to move out of the bohemian Latin Quarter of Paris into an impressive house near the fashionable Bois de Boulogne. He kept the house for the rest of his life, even while living in London. It no longer survives, but some of his first modern-life pictures, including *Jeunes femmes regardant des objets japonais* (no. 10), are almost certainly set in its richly decorated interiors. Japanese prints and objets d'art were all the rage with both French and British artists at this time, and Tissot was an avid collector.

From the outset the modern-life subjects show Tissot's love of beautiful clothes, especially women's dresses, elaborately flounced, frilled, and looking as though they are being worn for the first time. As Baudelaire observed, the details of fashionable clothing are central to the whole idea of the modern. Tissot presents dresses and the women who wear them as exquisite objets d'art, and of course love-objects, in themselves. He had an early introduction to the world of fashion: his home city of Nantes was a center of the

fig. 1. Caricature of Napoleon III, from *Vanity Fair*, September 4, 1869

fig. 2. Caricature of George Whyte-Melville, from *Vanity Fair*, September 23, 1871

textile industry, and both his parents were in the clothes business, his father a linen-draper and his mother a milliner. He was a dandy himself and enjoyed the kind of sophisticated, modish company he shows in his paintings. Since Paris was so closely identified with fashion—the world of high fashion was dominated at this time by the glamorous house of Worth—his attention to couture was to become a key part of his identity as the Frenchman in London.

His reasons for moving to London, which he did in 1871, were several. Among them was the keen anglophilia among his circle of fellow artists in Paris; from early in his career he had affected the English "James" over his given name of Jacques-Joseph. He and his friends associated Britain with artistic freedom: the British art world seemed less hidebound by academic conventions than the French. In London artists were not so forced to take sides, to be reactionary or rebellious; they were allowed to be themselves. The quirkiness that came naturally to Tissot was tolerated, even expected. Britain boasted a solid tradition of modern-life painting, from Hogarth in the eighteenth century down to the Pre-Raphaelites. There was also a great deal of money to be made from the rich industrialists who led artistic patronage. But the most immediate factor was the turn of events in France in the years 1870–71, which brought a disastrous war with Prussia, the siege of Paris, defeat, then bloody civil war

between the forces of a right-wing government and the revolutionary Paris Commune. Like almost every able-bodied man in the city during the siege, Tissot was enrolled in the National Guard, joining a company of sharpshooters called the *Eclaireurs de la Seine*. Later he seems to have supported the Commune and may have fled into exile partly to avoid the backlash after its suppression. More important, he must have calculated that his prospects of making a good living were now far better across the Channel. He also had friends there, including Whistler, who had been established in Chelsea for some years.

Another of Tissot's London friends was Thomas Gibson Bowles, in whose house he lived for a while after his arrival. Bowles ran the newly launched *Vanity Fair*, which described itself as "A Weekly Show of Political, Social and Literary Wares." The main attraction of the magazine was the caricature of some man of the moment that was printed in color in every issue. Tissot had already contributed sixteen caricatures while in Paris; during his London years he made forty-six more. The earliest are outrageous and rather ugly send-ups of their unfortunate victims, done from photographs and other existing portraits; but soon Tissot developed a subtler, more naturalistic approach, based on sketches made directly from the subjects (compare figs. 1 and 2). In some ways the change indicates the general direction of his art around the

fig. 3. James Tissot, *Too Early*, 1873, oil on canvas, 28 x 40 in., Guildhall Art Gallery, Corporation of London

time of his move. His portrait of Frederick Burnaby (no. 15), for instance, shows him developing into a wonderfully un-stuffy and original portraitist. Burnaby had helped get *Vanity Fair* off the ground, come up with its name, and contributed articles, so it is unsurprising that his likeness—painted for Bowles—hovers somewhere between a normal portrait and one of the magazine's famous caricatures. More broadly, the paintings that were to be the signature pieces of Tissot's London career present a wryly observant, *Vanity Fair*-like caricature of society at large. They are gentle comedies in paint, designed to make his viewers smile at their own vanities and foibles.

Among his more overtly comic pieces is *Too Early* (fig. 3). The embarrassingly punctual guests, shuffling their feet, wondering where to look and what to do with their hands, are ridiculous because they have made a social mistake. (Tissot was to use much the same central group to represent a family of gauche provincials in his later series *La Femme à Paris*.) But there is a deeper comedy to the situation, which is that they, their hostess, the guests yet to come, probably we the viewers too, should abide by the absurd conventions that make arriving early so uncomfortable. As in his other pictures of the leisured classes at leisure, Tissot ever so delicately portrays their social life as a ceremony in which the main object is to wear the right clothes and behave correctly. In *Hush!* (no. 39) the party is in full swing but no one seems to be enjoying themselves. Everybody is too concerned with appearing nonchalant—the blasé, slightly bored look was a vanity of the high life that Tissot always observed with relish—and the impending concert is quite clearly a bore: the only guests showing much interest are the two Indians on the right, and then perhaps more out of curiosity than love of the violin. The settings of *Too Early* and *Hush!* could well be the same house, upstairs and downstairs; typically, it is brand-new, with the most fashionable rococo-revival decorations. In London Tissot lived a life of some affluence himself, buying an impressive house in St. John's Wood. It was rumored among his old friends in Paris that he kept champagne on ice ready for any guests who might call, and a liveried servant in the garden to polish the leaves of the shrubs!

In many ways the centerpiece of Tissot's work in Britain, *The Ball on Shipboard* (no. 27) shows to a high level of refinement the irony that suffuses his portrayal of the fashionable, slightly questionable set who were his favorite stratum of British society. The ball is taking place during the week of the annual sailing regatta at Cowes on the Isle of Wight. Typically Tissot shows little interest in the particulars of place, focusing instead on the guests and their social interaction. The couples placed here and there on the decks lend the scene a hint of the *fête galante*, a distinctly French genre of painting showing episodes of courtship in an idyllic setting. Tissot may even have had in mind the most famous example, Antoine Watteau's *Pèlerinage à l'île de Cythère* (*Pilgrimage to the Island of Cythera*) (Paris, Musée du Louvre). The idea of equating the Isle of Wight with Cythera, the mythic island of love, might well have appealed to his sense of humor. Given the number of unattached young women at the ball, there may be flirtation and amorous possibility in the air, but again there are no smiles or laughter, nor even much conversation. The positions and gestures of the guests suggest disconnection rather than togetherness. Fixing his characters in immaculate isolation within the crowd, at a party they cannot leave—at least until the ship docks—Tissot surely intended his scene as a reflection on social life in general. Not that he would ever sermonize. He shows too evident a delight in beauty and pleasure, in his characters' finery and savoir-faire, for his meaning to be taken as disapproval. He mocks what he loves, maintaining a cool, dandyish detachment from the sophisticated set while reveling in every detail of its appearance and behavior.

Tissot had a kind of repertory company of models who appear and reappear throughout his London paintings. The elderly man with white whiskers and a boater in the center and the young woman with a fan in the left foreground of *The Ball on Shipboard*, for instance, appear together in the left foreground of *Hush!* He also kept a stock of clothes and props. The same young woman's striped dress, along with the outfit of the woman standing behind her leaning on the rigging, both recur in *London Visitors* (no. 23). Most remarkably of all, some of the outfits in *The Ball on Shipboard* appear more than once within that painting. The scene

fig. 4. James Tissot, *Boarding the Yacht*, 1873, oil on canvas, 28 x 21 in., private collection, courtesy of the Crane Kalman Gallery

contains three pairs of "twins" dressed identically: the pair in the boaters near the center, and those in pale blue and pale green, respectively, sitting together in the middle distance to the left; and the pink and brown ensemble worn by the woman ascending the stairs on the right reappears twice and possibly three times. This strange repetition may derive from fashion plates of the time, which often showed the same dress from different angles. At the beginning of his famous essay, Baudelaire considers a series of such images, finding in them "the moral attitude and aesthetic value of the time."[2] Is this touch of the absurd Tissot's wry comment on the conformity imposed by high fashion? On the rise of the ready-to-wear dress, which was a multiple rather than a unique creation?[3] On the socialite's nightmare of arriving at an event to find someone else in the same outfit? Perhaps it is meant to suggest the movements of the same woman to different parts of the ball over a period of time. Perhaps it is a piece of sheer mischief. No one has yet come up with a completely satisfactory explanation.

Foreign artists who have painted in London, from Canaletto to Claude Monet, have painted scenes on the Thames. Following the lead of his friend Whistler, for whom the industrial waterfront was a favorite subject, Tissot took a delight in river life in its most modern aspects. Typically, *The Thames* (no. 20) is a story of modern love with a playful, comic twist. The single man with a pair of attractive young women was his favorite cast of characters—it appealed to male fantasies and allowed more scope for complicated emotional drama than a couple—and in this case it is a sailor taking his lady friends for a pleasure-boat trip through the Pool of London, the busy stretch of dockland immediately downriver from the Tower. It would have been "fast" in the extreme for women to entrust themselves, unchaperoned, to the perils of a champagne picnic on the river with a young sailor. Whether they are a pair of sisters, friends, or merely rivals, the implication is that the sailor will be choosing one or the other as the object of an amorous advance. As if the situation were not suggestive enough in itself, a scantily clad figurehead above him seems to body forth his thoughts. Some of the humor in another of Tissot's comic-romantic nautical threesomes, *Boarding the Yacht* (fig. 4), lies in the

resemblance of the sailor to that stock figure of jokes about lechery, Henry VIII. With another, *The Gallery of H.M.S. Calcutta* (no. 28), the title is surely a bawdy reference to the curvaceous form of the young woman in the foreground, playing off the vulgar French pun "quel cul tu as!" (what an ass you have).

When Tissot showed *The Thames* at the Royal Academy in 1876, it attracted some of the worst—and most telling—reviews he was ever to receive. Its hedonism and suggestiveness struck the British critics as risqué, bordering on the outrageous. *The Times* called the subject "questionable material" and the *Athenaeum* found the painting as a whole "thoroughly and wilfully vulgar." As they had done before, the reviewers dwelled on the Frenchness of Tissot's work. Although the young women were "rather more acceptable types of *belles anglaises* than the disdainful misses the artist usually selects," remarked the *Illustrated London News*, "the supercilious air of the sandy-haired officer seems to smack of French satire." Even the *Graphic*, usually a supporter, described the work as "hardly nice in its suggestions. More French, shall we say, than English?"[4] Though generally favorable, the British response to Tissot was often tinged with resentment and could quickly slip into xenophobia. The humorous portrayal of British types might be all very well in the work of a native painter, but coming from a Frenchman it seemed more than a little presumptuous. Many suspected that Tissot might be making fun of them, of British manners and morals, even of Britishness itself, and they were probably quite right. It remains one of the delights of Tissot's art to see the Victorians through the eyes of a foreigner. He gives us the outsider's take on life and love in this most modern of modern societies, noticing what the British themselves took for granted, teasing them for their famous respectability and reserve, revealing—by the lightest of touches—that they too thought about sex.

The tradition of British modern-life painting, from Hogarth to the Pre-Raphaelites, was essentially a narrative tradition. Most British art aspired to the condition of storytelling—as Whistler was fond of pointing out with his jibes against "the British subject." Painters strove to tell the stories in which their characters were involved with maximum clarity, choosing just the right moment of action, spelling things out in gestures, facial expressions, and easily legible symbolism. With Tissot, by contrast, there is always an element of ambiguity, a tease. He delights in giving us hints toward some story line that might be unfolding in his pictures, but prefers to leave the possibilities open and tantalizing. If ever anything looked like a vital clue, it is that cigar on the portico steps in *London Visitors*. But who could say for sure what it means? And what of the gesture of the beautiful, bored young woman in the same picture, pointing with her umbrella toward Trafalgar Square? Tissot's women have their own sign language of accessories—fans, umbrellas, parasols, handkerchiefs, and gloves—yet what exactly they are saying remains mysterious; often they look directly at us, immodestly according to the manners of the time, as though daring us to try and read a message in their eyes.

A title might explain all, but Tissot's are rarely much help: indeed, he made a point of not giving too much away in them, changing them on occasion as though they were of no real consequence. We gain some insight into what he intended us to make of his ambiguities from his plan to have the etchings after the series *La Femme à Paris* accompanied by stories inspired by the images. For *La Menteuse* (*The Liar*), which shows simply a young woman holding some flowers and parcels in a finely decorated interior, his old friend Alphonse Daudet provided the story of an artist's mistress who comes home with gifts she claims are from people to whom she is giving piano lessons; only after her death does the artist discover she has been deceiving him. In much the same way, though not quite so elaborately perhaps, Tissot wishes us always to imagine what stories his characters might be playing out. If narrative content can be latent, optional, and largely the invention of the spectator, then his work is narrative—but that is hardly what most British artists would have understood by the term.

Tissot's flair for the suggestive mise-en-scène and the perfection of his technique, a form of Impressionism in miniature, have drawn attention away from his inventiveness in composition. The critic John Ruskin snootily wrote off his works as "mere coloured photographs." The disposition of

figures and spaces in a painting such as *The Ball on Shipboard* may appear casual, but in fact the work is a masterpiece of composition: a mass of color and detail, tending by its nature to confusion, is kept deftly under control. The empty floor space in the right foreground, moving away to the left, establishes a firm perspective and provides pictorial relief from the busyness elsewhere; in his carefully judged contrasts of spare and busy areas of design, Tissot learned much from the Japanese woodblock prints that he admired and collected. Meanwhile the apparently random cutting-off of figures at the left, a device borrowed from his contemporaries in the French avant-garde, particularly Degas, gives both a slice-of-life look and the hint that the scene continues beyond what is actually shown. The composition of *London Visitors* is similarly ingenious and daring, with the principal figures placed well off-center and large areas occupied by stonework. The effect is again that of a casual glimpse, although the play of horizontals and verticals and the alternation of tones are finely calculated.

In some ways Tissot's art reflects his life. At the most obvious level his moves from Paris to London and back meant that he painted French subjects, then British, then French again. More specifically, there is within his British work a change of mood that corresponds to the most important event of his personal life: his falling in love with Kathleen Newton. She was a beautiful Irishwoman, eighteen years his junior, whose marriage to a surgeon in the Indian Civil Service had ended in almost immediate separation and divorce. She moved into Tissot's house as his mistress shortly before or after giving birth to an illegitimate son, presumably his, in 1876. From this time onward, he was less gregarious, and in his paintings the worlds of society and fashion give way to domestic life, glittering balls to picnics in his garden, crowds of guests to intimate groups. For a time his favorite models—almost his only models—were Newton, her son Cecil, her daughter Violet, and her niece Lilian Hervey. Again and again this family group appears at leisure in the artist's garden, a private Eden in which Newton plays a modern, St. John's Wood version of Eve—not quite the respectable married woman that the suburban trappings might lead us

fig. 5. James Tissot, *Waiting for the Ferry*, c. 1878, oil on canvas, 10½ x 14 in., private collection

to expect.[5] In the two versions of *Waiting for the Ferry* (fig. 5 and no. 54), her brother Frederick sits in for Tissot himself in the role of the lover or husband.

Tissot's personality is elusive. There is little to go on, and much of what there is seems quite contradictory. He has been described as both cool and passionate, carefree and neurotic, arch and sincere, sophisticated and superstitious, sociable and reclusive. "This complex being," as one friend called him, may in some measure have been all those things all the time.[6] His art hardly suggests a simple, straightforward soul. The picture becomes a little clearer, however, when we consider the traumatic, transforming effect on him of Newton's death from consumption in 1882. He was forty-six at the time and so devastated by the event that, from this point on, he can almost be regarded as a different man and artist. His middle and old age were to be colored by a sometimes rather ludicrous devotion to spiritualism, through which he believed he could communicate with his beloved, and a religious fervor that strains credibility. Like a living allegory of sacred and profane love, he turned from parties and picnics to the pious recreation of stories from the scriptures.

Shortly after Newton's death he gave up his London home and moved back to Paris. The deeper changes were not so immediately apparent. For two or three years he pursued more or less the same artistic line as he had in London. Ambitiously he undertook a series of fifteen large canvases showing scenes from the lives of Parisian women, *La Femme à Paris*. He had always been skilled at involving the viewer in the action of his paintings, having characters look out at us as though aware of our presence, leaving clear spaces in the foreground, even empty seats, as though we were expected to walk in and sit down. In *La Femme à Paris*, he pulls out all the illusionistic stops. *La Demoiselle de magasin* (no. 67) puts us in the position of a customer leaving a shop, with an assistant smiling at us and holding the door open. Other works in the series feature a figure so close to us in the foreground as to seem part of the real rather than the pictorial world. Each scene is at some level erotic: the idea of the *Parisienne* implied sexual adventure in a world of modernity and style.[7] By careful choreography, through the body language of his characters, the lines of the composition, and the manipula-

tion of space, Tissot continued to suggest an atmosphere of veiled passion and amorous intrigue. What a tense and fascinating network of looks pass across the circus ring in *Les Femmes de sport* (no. 66), especially that of the clown toward the young woman who ignores him and looks out at us, the viewers. In that figure of the clown, dressed in a costume with a British flag across the chest, yearning—it seems—for some response from a beloved high above him, it is not far-fetched to see Tissot's self-image at this time.

His last *Femme à Paris* painting showed a fashionably dressed lady singing in duet with a nun during the Mass. While making sketches for the composition, having hardly set foot inside a church for years, Tissot had a vision of Christ and was filled on the spot with religious ardor. This is his own story, and it may be his poetic and dramatic way of describing a growing commitment to religion that began in his mental sufferings over Kathleen Newton's illness and death. During the last year of her life he painted a series of four powerful works that are modern but also religious, retelling the story of the Prodigal Son in contemporary dress and settings (see nos. 72–75). As well as pointing the direction his art was to take following his visionary experience, the series was at some level autobiographical. Like the Prodigal Son, Tissot had left his native country and lived abroad. He had certainly not frittered away his money in riotous living and sunk into poverty, but he might well have seen the wretchedness to which the Prodigal is reduced as an image of his own emotional distress. Having grown up in a strict Roman Catholic household and attended Jesuit college, then lived a faithless life—some would have said an immoral one—he might well have felt the need for repentance and redemption.

After the *Femme à Paris* series and a false start on a similar project to be called *L'Etrangère (Foreign Woman)*, Tissot in his fervor conceived the idea of producing a lavishly illustrated book of the life of Christ. This and the illustrated Old Testament that was its sequel occupied him for the remaining sixteen years of his life. As an age of religious uncertainties, in which modern scientific knowledge was undermining the authority of Bible and Church alike, the later nineteenth century had given birth to a new genre of religious art, one

that presented the events of the scriptures in insistently factual terms. The aim was not to create a vision of heavenly beauty and perfection, like a Madonna by Raphael, but a scientifically arrived-at testament to the truth of the given event and the characters involved—something that a Doubting Thomas of an age could believe in, and from which it could take much needed comfort. It was a largely British and Protestant phenomenon, and its leading practitioner was the Pre-Raphaelite painter William Holman Hunt.

Tissot's contribution was to apply the principle to biblical illustration on a scale never before attempted. He set great store by doing detailed research on the customs and dress of biblical times and visiting the sites in the Holy Land where the events he was depicting had taken place, bringing back hundreds of notes, photographs, and sketches. "For a long time," he announced, "the imagination of the Christian world has been led astray by the fancies of artists." He prided himself on setting the record straight, informing his astounded father, for instance, that Calvary was no great hill but "not more than from 20 to 22 feet high at the most."[8] But there was more to it than archaeology, for Tissot the spiritualist believed that the location of a spiritual event retained an aura that could influence the mind at the deepest level; some of his images of the supernatural, especially his angels, have a distinct air of the séance about them. He described his biblical designs as "not labor but prayer" and claimed to have made them in a kind of trance: as he attempted to draw Christ's face, his sketch would become blurred, and another image, the real face of Christ, would miraculously appear for him to trace. He made his designs in gouache and pen and ink; the originals were first widely exhibited in France, England, and North America, then reproduced in the books by lithographic and photomechanical processes. With their combination of realism and mysticism, they struck a powerful chord, attracting enormous acclaim and publicity on both sides of the Atlantic. According to one source, women seeing them in the traveling exhibition would sink to their knees and "crawl round the rooms in this posture, as though in adoration."[9]

Tissot is not the kind of artist who features largely in general histories of art. This is by no means because he is a forgotten figure. On the contrary, his work is admired, studied, and collected all over the world, sometimes with a cult-like devotion. Through greeting cards and other forms of mass reproduction it is familiar to a large public. What makes him easy to omit from the survey books is that he defies the normal categories: he was neither a leader nor a follower, neither academic nor avant-garde, an outsider in both the French art world and the British. His work is not in that supposed mainstream of style that flows through the nineteenth and twentieth centuries from Impressionism to Post-Impressionism and so on. Though trained in Paris and on close terms with Degas, he chose to live in London during the great years of the Impressionist movement; when invited to exhibit with the group, he declined. If he was interested in advanced painting of the 1880s and 1890s, he certainly never showed it. Perhaps most important, he was at his best in that mode so woefully undervalued in the visual arts, the comic. Our hope in this exhibition and the accompanying catalogue is simply to present him on his own terms, to bring out the intelligence, the inventiveness, and the humor that make him such a highly enjoyable artist.

Costume Pieces

Tissot himself left little account of his life or thoughts, but these have been reconstructed in some detail.[1] The son of a successful merchant and a shop assistant, he was born in Nantes in 1836. After an early interest in architecture, he decided to become a painter and moved to Paris in 1856 or 1857. Although he did enroll at the Ecole des Beaux-Arts, most of his artistic education occurred more informally, among a circle of avant-garde artists and writers in Paris. While training in the atelier of Ingres's pupil Louis Lamothe, he met Edgar Degas, also a student, who became a close friend. Other influential acquaintances were the painters Edouard Manet, Alfred Stevens, Ernest Meissonier, Alphonse Legros, Ferdinand Heilbuth, and, perhaps most important, James McNeill Whistler.

Tissot quickly achieved recognition in official circles. In 1859 he exhibited five of his pictures at the Salon, and at his next appearance, in 1861, one was purchased by the French State. Influenced by the early Italian art he had seen on a trip to Milan, Florence, and Venice, as well as by the work of the prominent Belgian artist Hendrik Leys (see fig. 6), these early Salon works were in a conservative, medievalizing manner. Their success convinced Tissot that historic subjects and a highly detailed imitation of the art of the past would lead to an illustrious career, despite critical attacks for plagiarism and affectation, and he worked in this mode until his abrupt shift to contemporary scenes at the Salon of 1864.

By setting his pictures in the past, Tissot was following the current aesthetic convention that a certain degree of distance—of either time or place—was necessary to make a subject truly "artistic." Unless depicted in a heroicizing or idealizing fashion, modern life was, by definition, outside the parameters of high art. The idea of the historical subject as a superior form was to prove tenacious; even after Tissot had become an artist of modern life, he was still drawn to distant eras and in 1868 began a series of works set in the Directoire period. Upon settling in England, he returned to images of the past in some of the first works he exhibited there—scenes of eighteenth-century lovers at taverns on the Thames—which proved very popular.

1   *Pendant l'Office (During the Service)*
     also known as *Martin Luther's Doubts*, 1860
     Oil on panel, 34¾ x 26¾ in.
     Signed and dated, lower left
     Exhibited: probably Salon, 1861
     Private collection

At a scene of prayer in a medieval church, a heavy stone pier separates the central male figure from a group of mainly female worshippers clustered in an odd, crowded pyramid to the left of the composition. Unlike those of the rest of the congregation, his hands are not brought together in devotion but merely crossed over his midriff, and his expression is troubled. To the far left is a candelabra bearing symbols of the transience of human life, mortality, and the tortures of hell: a winged hourglass, a skull and crossbones, a grave-digging spade, and a spiked tail. In the dirt below the stand are other candles, representing the precariousness of human existence on its shifting sands. These threats are offset by the promise of redemption and resurrection in the crucifix hanging above. In the background is a stained-glass window showing a dog, a traditional symbol of fidelity and the guidance offered by a priest to his flock. This contrasting symbolism presumably echoes conflicting beliefs in the mind of the main character.

The work illustrates the extent to which a title can inflect, or indeed entirely create, the meaning of the painting to which it is attached. The only certain contemporary title appears on an 1861 photograph: *Les Vêpres (Vespers)*, although the painting is probably the one exhibited at the Salon of that year as *Pendant l'Office*. By 1868 it was in a collection in Leeds, England, with the title of *Young Luther in Church*, and it was sold in 1886 as *Luther's Misgivings, in the manner of Leys*.[2] The connection to Martin Luther has been accepted, especially as the young man resembles Hendrik Leys's depictions of this historical figure. The fact that the picture seems not to have acquired its association with Luther until it was in England, however, may indicate that this was a Protestant reinterpretation of the image. For Tissot himself to risk offending the Roman Catholic Church by celebrating the founder of the Protestant Reformation would be odd at such a fragile stage of his career.[3]

On the other hand, possibly he did intend to depict Luther but avoided censure by giving the image a benign title, so that only those with inside knowledge would recognize the subject matter. At this time Tissot and Degas were young artists full of doubts of their own, as well as new ideas that would lead them to break with the teachings of the Ecole des Beaux-Arts in which they had trained, so Luther may have had personal meaning for them as an opponent of the Establishment.

no. 1

2 *Marguerite à l'église* (*Marguerite in Church*), c. 1860

Oil on canvas, 20 x 30 in.
Signed, lower right
National Gallery of Ireland, Dublin

Tissot drew his theme from Goethe's *Faust* as adapted and popularized by Charles Gounod's opera of 1859, in which the character of Gretchen is called Marguerite. In this narrative Dr. Faustus, who has contracted to serve the devil in the afterlife in return for perpetual youth, becomes infatuated with the pure and lovely Marguerite. With the help of Mephistopheles, he seduces and then deserts her. After having a child out of wedlock, whom she allows to die, Marguerite is shunned and taunted by her fellow villagers. In desperation she seeks solace in repentance and goes to a church, where the devil prevents her from entering by summoning visions of her former happy, blameless life. Struggling to preserve hope as demons whisper to her of the terrors of eternal punishment, Marguerite faints. Once she recovers, she finally rushes into the church to pray, the scene that Tissot shows us.

Tissot's interest in the story of Marguerite marks the first major appearance in his œuvre of a favorite theme, complicated or frustrated relationships between men and women. In many ways Marguerite resembles the penitent Magdalene, with whom Tissot would become fascinated in his New Testament illustrations. Abandoned by her lover, miserably aware of her sin, she sits on a bench near a shrine, her downcast gaze and dejected posture indicating her repentance. Her hand lies passively in her lap in self-forgetfulness, her elaborate costume bulking behind her. Unlike the small children, apparently outcasts themselves given their traveler's bundle, she lacks the innocence that would enable her to pray directly in front of the holy relic behind the metal lattice; instead she must sit off to one side, incapable even of bringing her hands together.

Compositionally the image is divided into two halves, with Marguerite on the cold flagstones and the children on the woven mat, underlining her alienation from their pure state.The painting over her head is a Last Judgment—with the kneeling Virgin at the left, the feet of Christ (seated on the rainbow) in the middle, and the lower part of the body of St. John at the right[4]—and this foreshadows the end of Marguerite's story: like the tonsured monk rising from a grave on the right, she is to be resurrected into heaven, ultimately triumphing over Mephistopheles. On Marguerite's dress are embroidered daisies (*marguerites* in French), symbolizing innocence, and over her head is a crest with three crescent moons, traditional sign of virginity, perhaps implying that her soul is stainless.

The work is one of several of Tissot's paintings based on the Faust legend. His interest in the story and the elements of medievalism in his style at this time derived in part from his admiration for Hendrik Leys, a Belgian painter who was attempting to regenerate the Northern school of art by looking back to the Flemish primitives. Leys had himself illustrated the Faust legend (fig. 6), which may have inspired Tissot's series.

Tissot's Faust paintings were not well received by the critics. They felt that drawing on early Northern painting in order to imbue French art with originality was unnatural and that the Faust legend was an outworn subject; by this time Marguerite had been depicted so frequently that one writer termed her "the eternal and banal victim of painters of our age."[5] Nevertheless Tissot received official recognition for his efforts when *The Meeting of Faust and Marguerite* (1861; Musée d'Orsay, Paris) was purchased from the Salon by the French State.

no. 2

fig. 6. Hendrik Leys, *Faust and Marguerite*, 1856
Oil on panel, 39¼ x 69¾ in.
Philadelphia Museum of Art
The William L. Elkins Collection

3   *Jeune femme en bateau* (*Young Woman in a Boat*), c. 1870
    Oil on canvas, 19 x 25 in.
    Signed, lower right
    Exhibited: Salon, 1870
    Private collection

Sitting in a moored skiff, a woman gazes pensively out at the viewer, her little finger subtly fretting at her lower lip in a coquettish gesture. Her broad-brimmed hat and vaguely eighteenth-century garment suggest the costume of the period just after the French Revolution, in which Tissot became interested around 1868 despite his recent conversion to modern-life subjects. Perhaps he hoped by this choice of a recognizably French past to silence the critics who had disliked his work in the style of the Belgian artist Leys. Unlike the serious, medievalizing images of a few years earlier, his pictures set in this period treat trivial subjects: picnics, boat trips, and riverside trysts. Here the pug adds a humorous note, absurdly acting as watchdog to his mistress. One reviewer snidely described her pet as "a dog with the head of a monkey…who appears without doubt to be a very rare species."[6]

Oddly the boat has only one oar, and the oarlock on the right is empty of the steadying pegs. The other oar is entangled in weeds, suggesting that the woman is stranded, or at least unable to leave this secluded bend of the river. When the picture appeared in England, a critic interpreted her expression as annoyance at being kept waiting by a lover: "There is anger in her soft eyes—a bull-dog squats behind, and is as impatient as she is with more of indignation in his expressive countenance."[7] A popular pastime for young couples, rowing down a stream together suggested the harmony necessary for a successful marriage. Such overtones of sentimental romance made rowing scenes a frequent subject in popular illustration, and the image of a young lady alone in a boat was a common subcategory of the genre. The caption to a wood-engraving of 1880 (fig. 7) explained that the woman looking out at the viewer expectantly was waiting for someone to row her boat for her, metaphorically suggesting her need of a husband.[8]

In this context, the flowers on the boat seat appear to be a love token. Indeed, Tissot signed the work on the board

fig. 7. "Down by the River," cover of the *Illustrated London News*, July 17, 1880

under the bouquet, as if he himself were the source of the flowers. In the way in which the woman could be looking either at the artist himself or at the viewer, *Jeune femme en bateau* represents an early example of Tissot's characteristic play with viewer identity, as well as his preoccupation with the potentially erotic charge of a woman's outward gaze.

Several small red-chalk sketches for this work demonstrate Tissot's careful working method. In the first, he blocked out the masses of the composition; in the next, he filled in the shading; in the final sketch, he drew a more complete image, apparently from life. Frequently he sketched the site of a picture and its model separately, sometimes completing watercolor studies as well.

YALE ONLY

no. 3

4 *Les Adieux (The Farewells)*, 1871
   Oil on canvas, 39½ x 24⅝ in.
   Signed and dated "1871 Londres," lower right
   Exhibited: Royal Academy, 1872
   Bristol Museums and Art Gallery

One of the first pictures Tissot painted after moving to London, this work depicts a man and woman in late-eighteenth-century dress separated by a green iron fence and gate, a barrier that emphasizes the pathos and perhaps the finality of their parting. Gazing intensely at the woman, who looks away in distress, the man rests his index finger on the sharp point of a railing; the imagined pain of this gesture represents his emotional pangs. His other hand, ungloved, holds hers in silent fervor, suggesting the bond between them that will remain despite the separation symbolized by the fence. Given the lady's simple dress, contemporary reviewers deemed her a governess, maid, or schoolteacher, so the obstacle to the couple's union is no doubt financial; a respectable middle-class woman would be reduced to wage-earning professions such as these only if she had no alternative.

The proliferating symbols of loss and parting in *Les Adieux* include the scissors dangling from the woman's waist, the autumnal foliage in the background, and the dead leaves underfoot. From the outset of his English career, Tissot was preoccupied with the theme of separation, partly because of its usefulness as a catalyst for storytelling. In pictures such as *Les Adieux* or *Goodbye (On the Mersey)* (no. 37), the motif of the parting, like the reading of a letter, requires viewers to locate the scene in a narrative; they must imagine prior relationships between the represented individuals as well as their future separation. Perhaps the great number of images on this theme produced by the artist during his first few years in London symbolized his own recent departure from Paris, by which he was strongly affected, and his new displacement in English society. In the case of *Les Adieux* the foliage suggests a happy ending: in the Victorian language of flowers, the foreground ivy would represent fidelity and marriage, the holly hope, foresight, and passion.

In a stylish gesture Tissot calls attention to his signature on the step by painting it in the same color and shape as the woman's hat ribbons. His panache was warranted; the picture was much admired at the Royal Academy. As though prompted by a critic's disparaging remark that it "looks as if painted for the engraver, so little would it lose by translation into black and white,"[9] John Ballin made a print after the work, which became very popular. The success of the print may have encouraged Tissot to begin making his own reproductive etchings, keeping both copyrights and profits to himself.

no. 4

5   *An Uninteresting Story*, 1878
     Etching and drypoint, 12⅜ x 8 in. (W. 32)
     Signed and dated in the plate, upper right
     Private collection

An old soldier in a riverside tavern recounts his exploits in an ancient campaign. Spread out on the table are maps showing towns fortified in the manner of seventeenth-century Dutch or French military engineering (perhaps the work of the famous Marquis de Vauban), as well as a fleet of ships. The demure but desperate boredom of the young lady in the oversized mobcap, combined with the happy absorption of the soldier as he expounds on the male world of military prowess, create the sort of comic situation that Tissot explored in his earlier English work. Despite its relatively late date, the etching is closely related to the first painting Tissot exhibited at the Royal Academy after he moved to London, the ironically titled *An Interesting Story* (fig. 8). Works such as this immediately advertised the artist's qualifications for depicting identifiably English genre scenes for an English audience.

Like other early pictures in England, *An Interesting Story* depicts the Thames-side areas of Rotherhithe or Wapping in east London. With this choice of setting, Tissot tapped into the English fondness for quaint, colorful depictions of London's river. Novelists such as Charles Dickens had set scenes in ancient riverside taverns, and numerous painters and illustrators had portrayed the swiftly vanishing, ramshackle picturesqueness of the Thames wharves and warehouses.[10] James McNeill Whistler had turned to the Thames to establish himself in the British art world, producing his "Thames Set" of etchings in 1859–61. As Tissot and Whistler had been friends since they met in Paris in 1861, Tissot may have been signaling his allegiance to and admiration for Whistler in his choice of Thames subjects, a fact recognized by reviewers who compared the two.[11]

The Thames was a proven, popular subject, and Tissot must also have guessed that his eighteenth-century vignettes would appeal to the English taste for "neo-Georgian" genre painting. This had been taken up with great success by the English painters John Everett Millais, Frank and Marcus Stone, George Dunlop Leslie, and others. Tissot's recreation of the period is somewhat loose: the furniture dates to about 1800 and the costumes to about twenty years earlier.[12]

Besides depicting an identifiable English location, Tissot added humor to his work, also calculated to appeal to his new audiences. As has been suggested, the pontificating gentleman may be related, in type if not in literal reference, to Uncle Toby in Laurence Sterne's comic novel *Tristram Shandy*.[13] A popular figure in Victorian painting, Uncle Toby obsessively reconstructs old battles and historic fortifications, boring anyone who encounters him with endless details of his military exploits. As a comedy, *An Uninteresting Story* lent itself to the type of narrative "reading" of painting that Victorian viewers were conditioned to practice. Tissot's early English pictures were easily legible, although he soon began to experiment with ways to make them harder to read.

fig. 8. James Tissot, *An Interesting Story*, c. 1872, oil on canvas, 22¾ x 29½ in.
National Gallery of Victoria, Melbourne

no. 5

La Vie moderne

Tissot exhibited his first two paintings of modern-life subjects in 1864 and seldom returned to historicizing scenes until the Bible illustrations of the end of his career. Given his association with avant-garde artists of the period, he would have been surrounded by exciting new ideas about the appropriate subject matter for high art. Influenced by the poet and critic Charles Baudelaire, who urged artists to seek beauty in everyday life, the painters Gustave Courbet, Edouard Manet, and Edgar Degas had begun to spurn scenes of history, religion, and mythology in favor of the mundane and the ordinary. They opposed long-standing academic conventions and sought to make their work quintessentially modern, emphasizing ephemeral elements such as fashion and contemporary social practices.

Tissot was well positioned to take up these new, distinctly urban notions. As a young and soon quite wealthy man-about-town, he observed firsthand the boulevard life of contemporary Paris, including both the fashionable and the illicit modern entertainments that formed a primary subject for the avant-garde. Well-educated and aware of contemporary realist literature (in his library were books by his friend Alphonse Daudet, Gustave Flaubert, and those acute, acidic observers of contemporary Paris, the Goncourt brothers), he enthusiastically embraced the art of modernity.[1] Broadening his aesthetic horizons in a way that was equally of the moment, his close companion James McNeill Whistler introduced him to Japanese art and objects, newly arrived in Paris. From Japanese color woodblock prints Tissot drew elements of design with which he began to experiment: tilted, rushing perspectives, flattened spaces, and asymmetrical compositions.

Despite his occasional dabblings in an Impressionist style (see, for example, his unfinished self-portrait, no. 14), Tissot continued to paint with an academic tightness of execution and great attention to detail. Clearly this was a conscious decision rather than lack of talent as his twentieth-century detractors maintain; much as he admired the work of his friends, he believed that his own style was equally suited to depicting modern scenes, perhaps even more so. Rather than timidly rejecting the emerging modernist vision, Tissot created his own unique, modern way of seeing, melding traditional artistic techniques with new subject matter and experimenting with conventions of narrative art in ways peculiarly his own. French patrons quickly began to purchase his work, and by 1868 he was earning 70,000 francs a year and had built a house on the fashionable avenue de l'Impératrice in the Bois de Boulogne.[2]

no. 6

6 *Portrait de femme* (*Portrait of a Woman*), c. 1860–61
   Etching, 8¾ x 6½ in. (W. 4)
   Signed with monogram in the plate, lower left
   Private collection

This is one of Tissot's earliest forays into the technique of
etching, which had been recently revived in France and was
becoming very fashionable. Clearly he was still learning to
create convincing shading and form; in passages such as the
woman's left shoulder, the outline hovers oddly over the lines
which sweep down from it, and the ruffles on her dress are
somewhat confused. Yet the sense of spontaneity achieved in
such details as the wisps of hair over her forehead and her
expression, which appears to be caught in transition to a
smile, demonstrates Tissot's ability to endow etching with
some of the freshness of a sketch. Fourteen years would
elapse before he seriously turned his hand to etching again,
when he did so primarily to reproduce his own paintings.

7 *Les Deux Soeurs; portrait* (*The Two Sisters; Portrait*), 1863
Oil on canvas, 82½ x 53½ in.
Signed and dated, lower right
Exhibited: Salon, 1864
Musée d'Orsay, Paris; Gift of Alfred Bichet

Carrying her bonnet and parasol, the elder sister wears a spray of flowers in her belt, suggesting that the pair have been interrupted in a casual, private stroll. Every detail of the costumes is carefully recorded, including the gauzy transparent neckline of the woman, echoed in childish form on the girl's bodice. Suggesting a thoughtful study of the harmony of tones, Tissot's use of color is a striking aspect of the work, his palette restrained to green, white, and black, with red accents.

That this picture created something of a scandal when first exhibited at the Salon illustrates the extent to which stultifying pictorial conventions dominated the institution. Its style caused confusion among an art-going public accustomed to the conventions of supposedly outdoor light effects rendered in studio environments. It was dubbed "the green ladies," perhaps in derisive reference to Whistler's *White Girl*, shown at the Salon des Refusés in the previous year. Under the influence of Gustave Courbet and the realist school, Tissot painted outside, *en plein air*, in order to observe the way light played through trees; he found it created a greenish cast over dresses that were actually white. As a defender of the artist declared,

> the bourgeois…find these women frightening because they have never observed the freaks and the mixtures of color. In leaving the Salon, all one has to do is to pass through the Jardin des Tuileries, and to see under the vault of the tall, clustered chestnuts, the particular color of the shadows which reflect in pale green on the promenaders and glaze all the colors of their clothes with green….We are so used to a false nature that we are hesitant to accept real nature.[3]

Yet the outcry surrounding the picture was not entirely about its color. As one critic sneered, fed up with Tissot's constant imitation of other artists, "today it is M. Courbet

fig. 9. Gustave Courbet, *Les Demoiselles des bords de la Seine*, 1857
Oil on canvas, 68½ x 78¾ in., Petit Palais, Musée des Beaux-Arts de la Ville de Paris

…to whom he addresses himself."[4] Clearly Tissot was courting comparisons to Courbet, whose infamous *Demoiselles des bords de la Seine* (fig. 9) had scandalized Salon viewers in 1857. The similarity of the settings of the two works has been noted before, but perhaps Tissot was even more daring than we have supposed. His elder sister so closely resembles the *demoiselle* lying in the foreground in Courbet's picture, interpreted at the time as a prostitute, that Tissot may have employed the same model—or at least found one as similar as possible. Depicting a model who had formerly posed for a prostitute as a chaste lady on a stroll with her little sister may have created anxiety for his audiences by exposing the workings by which studio props and models became "art." The appearance of the same model in both of the artist's exhibited works of this year (see no. 8) would have reinforced the point.

no. 7

no. 8

8   *Portrait de Mlle. L. L. (Portrait of Mlle. L.L.)*, 1864
    Oil on canvas, 48⅞ x 39⅜ in.
    Signed and dated "fév. 1864," lower right
    Exhibited: Salon, 1864
    Musée d'Orsay, Paris

Casually seated on a small table rather than on the more customary chair, a young lady in a striking red and black outfit gazes candidly at the viewer; although the initials "L. L." remain a mystery, she is recognizable as the same model who appears in *Les Deux Soeurs* (no. 7). As if to emphasize his originality, on the right Tissot includes an oddly sliced-off bergère chair, designed specifically to accommodate a woman's broad skirts; here, however, it holds a portfolio rather than the sitter for a portrait. Clearly, Tissot's first modern-life pictures exhibited at the Salon (this and *Les Deux Soeurs*) declare his intentions of doing something new. With an informality novel in portraiture, the girl's enticingly exposed pink slipper and the discarding of her crinoline "cage" so that she can perch on the table imply that she has been captured in a private moment in her own home. The interior the artist delineates with such care is decorated in the fashionable Louis XV-revival style of which the Second Empire was fond. The girl's black silk dress displays the latest trend in skirts, currently in transition between the hoop and the bustle; trimmed with bobble fringe, her stylish red "zouave" bolero jacket was couture's homage to the soldiers stationed in the French colonies.[5] The similarity between the jacket, the girl's spherical red earrings, and the white curtain to the left, also decorated with little balls, suggests a wry comment by the artist on the excessive ornamentation common in both fashion and interior design at the time. In an inscription unusual in his œuvre, Tissot included the month in which the work was painted— February 1864—insisting on the absolute novelty and up-to-dateness of his modern-life picture.

Tissot also plays cleverly with levels of artifice, painting sprigged wallpaper while including the "real" flower from which the paper could have been modeled in a glass next to the woman's hand. Similarly, he places a mirror, symbol of art's ability to replicate the world, on the back wall parallel to the picture plane. Under the mirror's frame he inserts a small print or *carte-de-visite* of what appears to be a Dutch child in old-fashioned costume. This is a classic trompe-l'œil technique to convince the viewer of the three-dimensionality of the image, but Tissot perhaps intended it also to refer to his own artistic development. The figure resembles the elaborately dressed characters of his medievalizing earlier work (see nos. 1–2), bringing to mind his much-criticized archaic style. In drab black and white, the tiny card contrasts with its colorful surroundings, reminding the viewer of the past with which Tissot has made a definite break.

Brilliantly observed details, such as the distinctive shadows cast by the bobbles over the girl's right hand and the way her cheek reflects the bright red of her jacket, demonstrate Tissot's attentive study of actual light effects, which he learned in part from his friend Edgar Degas.

9   *Une Veuve (A Widow)*, 1868
    Oil on canvas, 27 x 19½ in.
    Signed and dated, lower left
    Exhibited: Salon, 1869
    Private collection

Seated under a flowered trellis and surrounded by the busy clutter of a table laden with late-afternoon refreshments, an overturned parasol, and a beribboned wicker stand bearing a large bouquet, a young woman in black pauses in her embroidery to contemplate the end of her needle with an ambiguous expression. As a woman who has lost her husband while still in the full bloom of her youth, the widow occupies a peculiar category of femininity, somewhere between the two extremes represented behind her: a bored, fidgeting little girl and a contented elderly lady absorbed in her reading. Neither child nor old woman, the widow is clearly not resigned to a life of sewing among womenfolk. Tellingly, the tea tray contains wine or sherry, the long-handled spoons suggesting that the beverage has been sweetened with sugar; the presence of several glasses indicates that the widow has had stimulating company, perhaps the source of her restive state of mind.

This widow's behavior would have violated the elaborate, strict mourning etiquette of the nineteenth-century bourgeoisie. A woman in mourning was effectively quarantined from society, unable to socialize for the first several months or even leave the house except to go to church. Symbolizing a withdrawal from worldly pleasures, the enveloping black widow's weeds were originally modeled on the nun's habit.[6] Enticingly feminine aspects of the toilette, such as perfume and curls, were banned, as a grieving woman was supposed to render herself as unattractive as possible.[7]

Clearly Tissot's young widow does not follow such conventions. At the Salon one critic satirically remarked to her: "you wear mourning, the black goes well with your blonde."[8] He may have been comparing her to the well-known fictional widow who is the subject of one of La Fontaine's fables; despite her initial dolorous protestations that she will never think of a man other than her dead

fig. 10. Alfred Stevens, *Le Dernier Jour de veuvage* (*The Last Day of Widowhood*), 1873–74, oil on canvas, 36⅝ x 25¼ in., Musée Royal de Mariemont

husband, she is urging her father to act as matchmaker within a few months of her bereavement.[9]

Given the possibilities for humor, widows were popular subjects. In *Le Dernier Jour de veuvage* (fig. 10) the Belgian Alfred Stevens shows a widow admiring her reflection in a mirror and adorning herself with a white flower, a hitherto proscribed ornament. From underneath the table appears a winged Cupid, hinting that the widow is dreaming of romance as she beautifies herself, having forgotten the loyalty she owes to her late husband.[10] Similarly, in the background of Tissot's picture a sculpture identified as Edme Bouchardon's *Cupid Stringing his Bow* suggests that the young lady in black feels desire rather than grief.[11]

YALE AND QUEBEC ONLY

no. 9

10 *Jeunes femmes regardant des objets japonais*
    (*Young Women Looking at Japanese Objects*), 1869
    Oil on canvas, 28 x 20 in.
    Signed and dated, lower left
    Cincinnati Art Museum
    Gift of Henry M. Goodyear, M.D.

Two women, one in a white peignoir and the other in street-wear, gaze intently at a ship model in a collection of Japanese objects. The guest has not even removed her gloves and muff before viewing what we assume must be a prize addition to the collection. The red, black, and yellow wooden construction is a model of a vermilion trading ship, used for both entertainment and trade. With a small samurai figure perched on the back and several oars and a rudder projecting from it, the ship rests on an expensive Japanese brocade embroidered with traditional motifs of flowering plum, bamboo, and water. Under the fabric is a wooden box, possibly a shipping crate. For serious collectors the documentation of an object was extremely important, and the container in which a piece arrived was often displayed along with the piece itself.

The room into which we are looking is at an angle to our viewing position, and we are slightly outside the wall implied by the white bobble-fringed curtain to the left. A complicated floor pattern leads the eye to a colorful Turkish carpet, beyond which is an elaborate Japanese shrine of red and black lacquer with bronze and gold foil. Plants line the grillwork walls in profusion, and the multicolored ship and brocade serve to overwhelm the eye still further. In the lower left an eighteenth-century Chinese or Japanese ceramic bowl serves as a flowerpot for a fern.[12]

All of the Asian items were probably from the painter's own collection; he was a recognized connoisseur of Japanese art. The interest in Japanese prints, ceramics, fabrics, and decorative arts had been expanding since the West first encountered them on a grand scale in the 1862 International Exhibition in London; many artists, most famously Whistler, began in various ways to incorporate Japanese influence into their paintings. Tissot was clearly enamored of the theme of women admiring Japanese objects, as he repeated it in two other compositions with the same title; no doubt he was pleased to be able to show off his collection and his talents as a painter simultaneously.

Strangely, Tissot has set up puppets, rather than an idol, as the focus of worship in the shrine. The crisscrossed woodwork on its open door repeats in miniature the pattern of the wooden grille lining the interior of the room, suggesting that the women are themselves like dolls on an altar, displayed as part of a collection. Contemporary viewers drew this kind of comparison as well; one commented, "we seem to see two beautiful birds in their golden cage."[13] Though the women may view the Japanese objects, they are themselves objects to be viewed.

The image is extremely busy, with myriad details adding to the eye's confusion. Its all-inclusiveness led one viewer to remark, "our industrial and artistic creations can perish, our morals and our fashions can fall into obscurity, but a picture by M. Tissot will be enough for archaeologists of the future to reconstitute our epoch."[14] With his gift for harmonizing colors, Tissot unifies the work despite its proliferating detail, skillfully keeping his palette to the colors of the central object: white, red, yellow, and black.

no. 10

Souvenirs du siège de Paris

This group of etchings is Tissot's artistic recollection of his experiences defending Paris in the Franco-Prussian War. On September 6, 1870, France became a republic after revolutionary forces deposed the Emperor Napoleon III. Shortly thereafter the Prussian (German) army besieged Paris, where hasty fortifications and ramparts were erected as citizens attempted to defend the city. According to Thomas Gibson Bowles, Tissot's friend and companion during the siege, there were 500,000 soldiers in Paris alone. In his role as war correspondent to the *Morning Post*, Bowles wrote a series of letters about the war that were published in book form —with illustrations by Tissot—as *The Defence of Paris, Narrated As It Was Seen* (1871).

The city was ill-prepared for such an attack, and many inhabitants believed until the last minute that peace negotiations would triumph. Few could imagine Paris "being actually reduced to occupy itself with anything more serious than pleasure."[15] Rather than fighting, the Parisians remained entrenched within the city as the Prussians attempted to starve them out, and were reduced to eating their pet dogs and cats, as well as more exotic zoo animals such as elephants, camels, and wolves. Finally the French surrendered. The left-wing Paris Commune was established in March 1871, only to be defeated in May 1871 and its proponents punished or executed. Tissot's summary departure to Bowles's home in London at this time suggests he felt himself in danger, and his involvement in the Commune has long been a subject for debate.[16] Since Bowles makes his opinion of the Communards as untrustworthy, scheming radicals very clear, it seems unlikely that he would have given Tissot shelter had the artist truly been associated with this group.

Later, in England, Tissot considered there might be a market for visual memories of a conflict still fresh in the public's mind and produced a total of six etchings of the subject.

11 *The First Killed I Saw*, 1876
   Drypoint, 17⅞ x 11⅝ in.
   First state, before the plate was cut down (W. 19, I/II)
   Signed in the plate, upper right
   Private collection

The soldier lies outside a wall of fortifications, probably having fallen from his post at the loophole cut through the wall. A temporary screen of rougher-hewn stones has been thrown together to protect the lookout but to no avail. Tissot subtly evokes the violence and bloodiness of warfare by forcing the viewer to retrace the trajectory of the soldier's fall: the rocky path to the left suggests a cascade down which he has plunged. The most darkly etched areas are on the soldier and in the black patch under his head, which pools like blood, while the jagged hole in the wall suggests the unseen wound in his body. Tissot's print echoes Bowles's description of this very site the next day: he saw "terrible spectacles of dead men, hideous ruins of God's creatures, lying in dark, black patches of gore," yet with "calm and almost placid expression, as though death had soothed while it struck them."[17]

The drypoint is taken from a drawing that Tissot did from life at the battle of the Château Malmaison, and according to two sources the man killed was a sculptor friend. Tissot's dispassionate transcription of the scene supposedly angered Degas, who believed that he should have reverently removed the body rather than sketching it.[18] Bowles recounts meeting Tissot, who was in the infantry group called the *Eclaireurs de la Seine*, on October 21, 1870; the artist told him of his experience lying in a field firing into a cloud of smoke without any idea of the proximity of the Prussians; seventeen of Tissot's company of sixty were killed or wounded.[19]

Tissot's depiction of war and its consequences takes its place in a long history of such images. They traditionally glorified battle, but Tissot's grim, realist treatment of the subject seems to echo the pacifist sentiments of Bowles. "These are the sights I should like to keep for the princes and rulers who delight in war," he wrote in *The Defence of Paris*.

no. 11

"The high-sounding military phrases of dispatches, and the nonsensical accounts of losses, convey very vague ideas; but it is when one finds oneself face to face with the individual man…that the misery of the thing really comes home to one."[20]

12   *The Green Room of the Theatre Française*, 1877
      Etching, 15 x 10⅞ in. (W. 27)
      Signed in the plate, lower left
      Private collection

During the Franco-Prussian War, many public buildings
became temporary military installations; the Comédie-
Française, shown here, was used as a hospital. In Tissot's
depiction the grand hallway of the theater, with its stately
recession of repeating window bays and bust sculptures on
pedestals, is abruptly truncated, the pictorial awkwardness
reminding the viewer of the unnatural use of a space
intended for elegant entertainment. The makeshift ward
contains two wounded soldiers battling the boredom of
recovery, one with a newspaper, the other with a cigarette.
On the wall to the left a red cross has been crudely drawn;
at one point Tissot seems to have been a stretcher bearer
for the Red Cross, and he may have encountered this scene
during his work.[21] In the foreground a tray of food awaits a
patient on an empty bed where Tissot has signed his name,
suggesting his empathetic presence among the wounded.
Over the gallery loom busts of French writers, their dignified
irrelevance pointing up the exigencies of war, in which there
is no longer a place for art, literature—or theater.

no. 12

13   *Grand'garde*, 1878
     Etching and drypoint, 10⅝ x 7⅝ in. (W. 42)
     Signed and dated in the plate, lower right; signed in pencil,
        lower left; red monogram stamp, lower right
     Private collection

This etching relates directly to a drawing Tissot made for
T. G. Bowles's *The Defence of Paris*. A lone soldier stands
watch at a makeshift fortification, clearly thrown together
from straw, earth, and pieces of lumber. In the distance is a
small summer house or other outbuilding on a grand estate
or park. The shutters leaning across the ditches suggest the
ruin of the glittering city of Paris even as they add a note of
reality; in his report Bowles recounts gathering shutters and
other pieces of wood with Tissot to make a fire.[22] Apparently
they originated from the building in the distance, or one similar to it, illustrating the way in which war reduces civilization to essentials: the shutters have returned to mere wood.

   The winter of 1870–71 was unusually cold, and many
French troops froze to death; Tissot realistically portrays this
soldier wrapped in a blanket. His pose, with one foot resting
higher than the other, was traditionally used by artists to
depict heroic military leaders, but Tissot has adapted it to
convey the determination of the common soldier.

   As with many of his etchings, Tissot signs the work
effectively in triplicate. First he affixed his mark as an artist,
etching his name into the plate ("J. J. Tissot 1878"), then he
added his pencil signature to indicate that he approved of the
impression, and finally he applied a red monogram stamp
in emulation of Japanese printmakers. In general, prints with
all three markers of authorship are most prized by collectors,
although Michael Wentworth has pointed out that Tissot's
application of his various signatures seems to have been
somewhat random, and that only the pencil signature was
a true indication of his assessment of a print's quality.[23]

no. 13

Men of the Age

Tissot is best known as a painter of women, and in his scenes from modern life he concentrated for the most part on representations of femininity. Rarely did he turn his attention to depicting men alone, and then usually for commissioned portraits. As portraits were a crucial means of support for a young artist still establishing himself, Tissot had to prove that he was capable of portraying masculinity or risk his talent being labeled weak and effeminate, suitable only for ladies. With the prestigious commission of 1868 to paint members of an aristocratic men's club in *Le Cercle de la rue Royale* (private collection), he demonstrated his abilities, and his success as a portraitist was assured. Tissot was clearly most comfortable depicting men from the upper and upper-middle classes, the status he sought for himself, and he portrayed them in luxurious interiors that echoed or illustrated their characters.

That hallmark of portraiture, the outward glance, makes Tissot's portraits of men easy to recognize as such; when he shows women in this way, however, the context is usually one of his modern-life genre scenes rather than a portrait. By the same token, the men in his genre pictures almost never meet the viewer's gaze. The marked discrepancy is curious, implying that the artist saw the relationship between men and representation in a different light from that between women and representation. Perhaps for Tissot women were symbols of his paintings themselves, their expressive, oblique, or appealing gazes embodying the way the picture itself solicited the viewer's attention: women *became* the paintings, in a sense, whereas men were active agents within the world the paintings illustrated.

no. 14

14 *Self-Portrait*, c. 1865
   Oil on panel, 19⅝ x 11⅞ in.
   Signed, lower right
   Fine Arts Museums of San Francisco
   Mildred Anna Williams Collection

This sketchy portrait has a striking immediacy that Tissot's more finished works lack. Perhaps influenced by the increasingly loose handling of Manet and Degas, he left the picture in this state rather than working it into a formal portrait. With his head in his hand, the young artist gazes somewhat ironically into the mirror, as his other hand, outside the picture space, transcribes what he sees. At this point in his career Tissot was experiencing the first flush of success, and his direct look conveys the confidence of a young man certain he will make his mark on the world.

In appearance Tissot was dark-haired, with wide-set brown eyes and a square jaw. He cultivated the manners and dress of a bourgeois gentleman rather than a bohemian artist, a significant decision given that artists were only just becoming respectable members of society. Born the son of a merchant, he clearly wished to rise in social status through his profession. Edgar Degas's portrait of him during his years in Paris (fig. 11) cleverly depicts his dual persona of gentleman and artist by placing him in a studio but not actually painting. The hat and cloak draped over the table suggest a wealthy *boulevardier* who has dropped into an artistic milieu for a casual, brief visit. The slender stick he holds also indicates Tissot's double nature: although thin and fragile enough to be a painter's maul stick, it also could be a walking cane, an elegant bourgeois attribute.

Degas may also be referring to the relationship between himself and Tissot. The gilt-framed picture at the top of the compositional pyramid (where Tissot's head would be in a conventional portrait) is a portrait of Frederick the Wise then thought to be by Lucas Cranach. As Theodore Reff has noted, Degas alludes in this way to Tissot's interest in early Northern art.[1] He might have inserted the work as a private

fig. 11. Edgar Degas, *James Tissot*, c. 1868, oil on canvas, 59⅝ x 44 in. The Metropolitan Museum of Art, New York. Rogers Fund, 1939

joke. Frederick the Wise was the patron of Cranach and the champion of Martin Luther; Tissot was apparently Degas's patron at the time—he was certainly the more successful and fashionable artist—and perhaps Degas looked to him to champion the "heretical" tendencies of the avant-garde.

15 *Captain Frederick Burnaby*, 1870
Oil on panel, 19½ x 23½ in.
Signed and dated, lower left
Exhibited: International Exhibition, London, 1872
National Portrait Gallery, London

Seated on a sofa draped in white fabric, Burnaby assumes a relaxed, informal pose, his legs crossed and stretched out in front of him. The deep blue and bright red of his military uniform dominate the composition, particularly in their striking contrast in the long stripe down his leg. His left arm rests along the sofa, his hand casually holding a cigarette in the center of the composition. On the wall behind him hangs an unrolled map, under which sits his full dress uniform: a cape, a plumed silver and gold helmet, riding boots, and a highly polished breastplate.

Burnaby was an acquaintance of the artist's close friend Thomas Gibson Bowles. The portrait was commissioned by Bowles, possibly in gratitude for Burnaby's assistance in establishing his magazine *Vanity Fair*.[2] Well-known for his enormous physical strength and his hot-air balloon experiments of 1864, Burnaby was a popular member of the Royal Horse Guards (or "Blues"), the cavalry regiment that protected the monarch; he eventually rose to the rank of colonel. Apart from performing feats of courage and bodily prowess, Burnaby wrote letters for *Vanity Fair* about his travels from Paris to Spain and later published several memoirs.[3]

Tissot's picture cleverly blurs the line between formal portraiture and genre painting. Although Burnaby is the focus of the image, the traditional signs of portraiture are not all present. Tissot does not place the figure in the center of the canvas, nor does he emphasize his individual facial features; his body and the details of the interior are as much a part of the image as his carefully waxed mustache. Burnaby does not look at the viewer, but off to the right and up, as if at someone standing just out of our view. Instead of memorializing his sitter in a static, permanent pose, Tissot has caught him with his lips parted in conversation; in so doing, he flouts the academic convention that a momentary pose was inappropriate to the solemn purpose of portraiture.[4]

fig. 12. Photograph of Burnaby, frontispiece to his book, *On Horseback through Asia Minor*, 1877

The picture is clearly more than an anecdotal image of a soldier. The books on the sofa and the pieces of armor serve as the captain's attributes, representing his intellectual and physical pursuits much as a palm frond or wheel identified a medieval saint. The map covers large portions of the British Empire, including Perim and Aden in the Red Sea, the Seychelles and several other islands in the Indian Ocean, India, Ceylon, Singapore, Hong Kong, Australia, and New Zealand. The Suez Canal, indicated in the upper left corner, had opened in 1869 and become a source of imperial conflict; Egypt's shares in it, coveted by Britain, were to be purchased by Prime Minister Disraeli in 1875.

The presence of the map suggests the part played by the Horse Guards, including Burnaby himself, in the establishment of this imperial territory. The Blues were the privileged elite of the British military, receiving higher pay, finer lodgings, longer leaves of absence, and better postings. Not surprisingly, many of its officers were from the aristocracy or extremely well-connected (Burnaby himself was a member of the Prince of Wales's circle) and had purchased their commissions rather than obtaining them through merit-based promotions.[5]

no. 15

Given the fact that he is lounging with crossed legs and smoking a cigarette, activities forbidden to gentlemen in the presence of ladies, we assume that Burnaby is in an exclusively male space.[6] In this regard, he embodies a particular masculine ideal of the period, that of the soldier who joins an exclusively male coterie in order to ensure the safety of the home he has left behind. In the nineteenth century the soldier represented a distillation of what were deemed essentially male traits, notably strength, fearlessness, and aggression.

Yet Burnaby's relaxed elegance belies this rugged notion of masculinity. In comparison with other portraits of him, in martial readiness with sword and military decorations,

Tissot's image is un-heroic; even its small size works to defuse its subject's renowned physical presence and strength. Here the captain wears his "undress" uniform, his hard, glinting armor cast aside, clearly in a social rather than a physical or violent situation. He represents not the "brute strength" model of masculinity but the contrasting one of gentlemanliness. His arms laid aside for the time being, he concentrates on refining his nature through education, represented by the books on the sofa, elegant grooming (the waxed mustache), civilized tastes (the cigarette), and entertaining conversation. His pallor, apparently true to Burnaby's actual looks, also points to his status as a gentleman.[7]

16   *M. le Capitaine* ✶ ✶ ✶ (*Gentleman in a Railway Carriage*), c. 1872
Oil on panel, 25 x 17 in.
Signed, upper right
Exhibited: International Exhibition, London, 1872
Worcester Art Museum. Alexander and Caroline Murdock De Witt Fund

Hanging on to the strap in a swaying railway carriage, the traveler shrewdly considers us. Although his identity is unknown, clearly he is the quintessentially modern gentleman, self-composedly gazing at the stranger seated opposite him while checking his watch. His gesture reminds us of the new importance of time in the railroad era. By collapsing distances and travel times between places and by systematizing time itself (prior to mid-century, each town and region had had its own time zone), trains played an important part in the creation of a "modern" consciousness.[8]

Perhaps responding to criticism that modern dress could not be aesthetic, Tissot plays inventively with the formulae of grand-manner portraiture. The fur trim and bulk of the captain's coat recall the rich dress of a Renaissance potentate such as Charles de Solier in a portrait by Holbein (fig. 13). In both pictures the gold chain symbolizing the social status of its wearer stands out distinctly from the surrounding fur-laden garments. Draping the lap rug over the gentleman's trousers further helps Tissot tackle the nineteenth-century portraitist's dilemma of painting contemporary costume. Yet while the intent of many traditional portraits was to fix their sitters in a timeless environment, preserving them for eternity, Tissot emphasizes the specifics of the time and place in which his sitter lives.

The man's right hand is gloveless, each nail carefully delineated, calling attention to the odd gesture with which he delicately clings to the carriage strap. Without the prop the gesture resembles that of the traditional Christian blessing. Although this may seem to be an unlikely allusion, two of Tissot's *Vanity Fair* caricatures depicted popes performing this very gesture, and in a late self-portrait, *Portrait of the*

fig. 13. Hans Holbein, *Charles de Solier, Sieur de Morette*, 1534–35
Oil and tempera on panel, 36½ x 29¾ in., Gemäldegalerie alte meister, Dresden

Pilgrim (no. 86), painted to accompany his New Testament illustrations, Tissot himself blesses his readers. In sly blasphemy, then, a bourgeois gentleman in fur coat with a pocket watch and guidebook becomes a modern-day messiah, a new prophet, blessing the viewer and sanctioning the values of modernity.

YALE AND BUFFALO ONLY

no. 16

17 *Algernon Moses Marsden*, 1877
Oil on canvas, 19½ x 29 in.
Signed and dated, lower right
The Old House Foundation Ltd.

Holding one knee and leaning casually against the back of an armchair draped with a tiger-skin, Marsden favors the viewer with a measuring glance. The setting is apparently Tissot's own studio—as in *Hide and Seek* (no. 57) but seen from a different angle. Marsden is clearly at ease in this domestic environment filled with luxury goods, including a Chinese porcelain lamp and Japanese jars on the table in the background, and his pose suggests familiarity with the painter.

The son of a merchant tailor and shipper, E. Moses, Marsden had formed a partnership for a year with his father before he struck out as an art dealer with the Conduit Street Gallery. His choice of a profession of higher status than his father's may have been what prompted him to change his name to Algernon Moses Marsden; perhaps he wanted to escape what he perceived as the taint of trade in his background.

A nineteenth-century phenomenon, the art dealer was becoming a vital intermediary between patrons and artists. Marsden was Tissot's own dealer at this time. In painting a portrait of him, which was most likely commissioned since it remained in the Marsden family, the artist acknowledged the commercial as well as the sentimental ties between them. Marsden may have chosen the site for this very reason, commemorating a personal as well as professional visit to the studio. Tissot shared his dealer's desire to improve his social status and, always conscious of appearances, had designed his atelier to resemble a luxurious drawing room rather than a place of manual labor.

Unfortunately Marsden appears not to have been as savvy a businessman as Tissot and ruined himself through high living. Tissot hints at his extravagant tastes through his large gold signet ring, finely manicured fingernails, cigar, and well-groomed hair and beard. The newspaper bankruptcy columns mention him with some frequency throughout the late nineteenth and into the early twentieth century. Married at twenty-four, he claimed he found it difficult to provide for his wife without gambling to supplement his income as a dealer. By 1881, employed by the King Street Galleries, he had accumulated debts of £6,218 and had assets of only £2,825. This particular bankruptcy was annulled a year later because the claimant, a family member (perhaps his father), settled with him. But by 1887 he was in court again, with £1,295 in debts and only £20 in assets. This, he declared, was due to "an excess of expenditure over income" and to gambling at the racetrack, at which the registrar hearing the case wryly rejoined, "our national love of sport." Obviously a charming and witty man, Marsden said that when money came in he "got rid of it" by gambling, described his profession as a dealer as "a peculiar and speculative one," and confided that it was always a "fluke" to get hold of a man with money; this sally occasioned a laugh from the court.[9]

Marsden also admitted in court to spending several weeks accumulating debt at Eastbourne, a fashionable resort. He was a dog lover and frequently exhibited his pets, occasionally collecting prize money but never enough to maintain his household. In 1901, once again bankrupt, he listed himself as a merchant living in the City, having returned to his father's profession after all.

YALE ONLY

no. 17

On the Thames

Having fled to London as an exile from Paris after the fall of the Commune in 1871, Tissot was intent on retrieving his lost artistic, social, and financial status. He wasted little time in finding patrons and building a career in London to rival the one he had left behind, having shown some foresight by exhibiting at the Royal Academy in 1864. Tissot remained in England from 1871 to 1882, graduating from being a guest in the house of Thomas Gibson Bowles, to living in a semi-detached villa in St. John's Wood, and finally to purchasing a freestanding home (also in St. John's Wood) with a large garden. He had a large circle of influential friends, including the artists George du Maurier, John Everett Millais, Albert Moore, James McNeill Whistler (at least until the infamous Whistler-Ruskin trial, when Tissot refused to testify on his behalf), Seymour Haden, Lawrence Alma-Tadema, and Giuseppe de Nittis.[1]

In 1874 Tissot seems to have been officially cleared of any association with the Commune, and from that point on he occasionally returned to Paris for short trips. The fact that he did not at this point move back permanently to his native land shows that his stay in London was more than a default option. Most likely he saw more opportunities for critical and monetary success in London than in Paris, where he may have returned to a reputation ruined by suspicions of his Communard activities. Much of his work in London represented a carefully considered strategy, and in a conscious appeal to his new patrons he chose to set his first English paintings on the river Thames.

Tissot's Thames-side works show a range of sites, from Gravesend in the east to Nuneham Courtney in the west. In creating a body of work unified by the theme of England's major river, he laid claim to a subject literally and figuratively at the heart of the country. Historically significant as a major transportation artery, the Thames grew increasingly vital to British industry and commerce in the nineteenth century. Because of its dual importance in both trade and travel, it was uniquely important to Britons, who held it almost in reverence.

Ironically, by choosing such a preeminently English locality as the Thames, Tissot exacerbated controversy over the nationality of his art; informed by particular conceptions of "Frenchness" and "Englishness," this debate was to haunt the rest of his career. Despite his apparent attempts to cater to English taste, critics throughout his London career labeled his works "French." In part this referred to aspects of his painting technique; his work was perceived as oddly "black and white," for instance, owing to his use of white paint to create an overall uniform appearance, a technique favored by French artists including Eugène Boudin and Claude Monet.[2] As an academically trained artist, Tissot also possessed a mimetic virtuosity rarely seen in English art, except perhaps among the Pre-Raphaelites.

More generally, French style implied French moral content, which was perceived by the English as dubious. Although they admitted that French artists were more technically adept and admired their rigorous and highly structured system of art education, British critics often accused them of masking a hollow or corrupt sensibility with an alluring appearance. This attitude derived from the British belief that the French themselves were vain, insincere, frivolous, and licentious.

The reception of Tissot's early English work, then, took place in the context of perceptions of his nationality. Despite his attempts to accommodate his work to English audiences in terms of subject matter and sensibility, it was scrutinized carefully for signs of potentially dangerous foreign qualities.

no. 18

18   *The Captain's Daughter*, 1873
      Oil on canvas, 28½ x 41¼ in.
      Signed and dated, lower left
      Exhibited: Royal Academy, 1873
      Southampton City Art Gallery

The young man taking a glass of spirits with the older gentleman seems to be listening to advice on his prospects with the lady, presumably the eponymous heroine, who turns her back on them. Given the dour and disappointed expressions of the two men, and the apparent lack of concern on the part of the woman, the courtship does not seem to be going smoothly. Apparently she would rather gaze at the shipping on the river with her binoculars than flirt with a sailor. Lying on the table and pointing to the object of the young man's desire is another, contrasting visual instrument, a telescope decorated with the recently invented International Code of marine signals, the colored flags used in maritime communication.

In this intricate composition Tissot creates a series of rhymed forms: the horizontals and verticals of the wooden rails, ships' masts and spars, and window panes; the lines of the men's legs and the woman's arms and body echoing the diagonal supportive struts of the docks. A sketch for the picture indicates that Tissot altered the composition to reinforce the woman's lack of participation in the male conversation; whereas her lower body was at first to be angled toward them, in the final painting she faces entirely away. Divided by the vertical supports of the balcony overhanging the river in the background, the male and female spaces remain separate, the rigid horizontals and verticals of the composition mirroring the complications keeping the young couple apart.

When first shown at the Royal Academy, the painting was mistakenly given the title of another Tissot in the same exhibition, *The Last Evening* (fig. 14). From descriptions in reviews it is fairly clear that the two titles were accidentally switched. Certainly when the dealer Agnew's purchased the present painting from the artist in 1873, it was with the title of *The Captain's Daughter*.

fig. 14. James Tissot, *The Last Evening*, 1873
Oil on canvas, 28½ x 40½ in.
Guildhall Art Gallery, Corporation of London

19 *Autumn on the Thames (Nuneham Courtney)*, c. 1875
Oil on panel, 29¼ x 19¼ in.
Signed, lower right
Private collection

On the river's edge a woman adjusts her scarf, her skirts blowing in the stiff breeze, while a man holds a small boat close to the bright green bank. On the boat a younger girl admires the water, her red hair streaming. Tissot leaves us confused as to whether the group has just arrived or is departing; to the left are three oars and a punting pole, which rests on a white parasol, but these clues could support either reading.

Near Oxford, Nuneham Courtney was a popular tourist destination, favored for picnics. Nuneham itself was the country seat of the Harcourt family, famed for its landscape garden laid out by Capability Brown. In season it was crowded with pleasure-seekers who punted or rowed up the Thames. Here autumn has colored the forest in the distance; in a rare concentration on landscape details, Tissot renders the many-hued trees and their reflection on the water with deft assurance, particularly where the reflection shades into that of the sky on the left.

Tissot depicts the pastoral, idyllic aspects of the river celebrated by many writers and poets and, like them, emphasizes the lush green foliage, breezy clean air, clear water, and abundant fauna. London's river and its banks had long been a popular subject for art, treated either topographically—by the Venetian view-painter Canaletto, for instance—or in a more Romantic vein by J. M. W. Turner and others. In the middle of the nineteenth century, stimulated by the establishment of river steamers offering quick, cheap transport, tourism along the Thames became a more common practice. Like the Impressionists, who painted in the Parisian suburbs along the Seine, Tissot followed in the tourists' footsteps, and the collective catalogue of his Thames works resembles a recommended itinerary in one of the new guidebooks.[3]

Although this work has previously been dated 1871–72, it is more likely from the period between 1874 and 1876, when Tissot was employing the blonde model in the foreground; she also appears in *Quarrelling* (no. 43).

no. 19

20 *The Thames*, c. 1876

Oil on canvas, 28⅝ x 42¼ in.
Signed, lower right
Exhibited: Royal Academy, 1876
Wakefield Museums and Arts

A man and two women lie on the rear deck of a steam launch in the Pool of London, site of the city's great docks. Nestled in the foreground is a picnic hamper full of plates and utensils; a large black and tan dog rests against the man's legs, while a small pug sitting between the two women peers at us, its tongue lolling out. On the extreme left is a craft peculiar to the river Thames, a hay barge, which with its distinctive red sails would have reminded the contemporary viewer of the specific location. In the distance to the left is a paddle steam ferry or tug, and behind it a sailing vessel. Directly behind the woman wrapped in the red-and-black-plaid blanket is a Blackwall frigate, towed by a steam tug and flying the red ensign of the Merchant (or commercial) Navy.

In contrast to Tissot's first Thames-side compositions, which were well received, this work disturbed contemporary audiences. Tellingly one reviewer pronounced, "the picture is washed out, yet dirty in colour, and, as to the choice of subject, it will be felt by most people that what happens to be disagreeable in nature needs no repetition in art."[4] Rhetoric about "dirty" painting in Victorian art criticism often represented a displacement of anxieties about the work as *morally* dirty.

Many reviewers dwelled on the polluted appearance of the scene, which contributed to their anxiety. "Mr. Tissot…who began with sunny prospects," commented one, "ends in the Thames with umbrellas and steam funnels belching out smoke."[5] Frequently described as a "plague," with all the accompanying connotations of disease and contagion, the filthy air of the city was a very real concern for social reformers, who believed it symbolized the unnatural, unhealthy aspects of urban life.[6] Tissot's depiction of the water was similarly troubling. The Thames, and particularly the Pool, had become so fouled with sewage and industrial waste that

in 1876, the year in which Tissot's painting was first exhibited, Parliament passed the Rivers Pollution Prevention Act.

The problem was compounded by the fact that the man with whom the women recline so indecorously was of dubious respectability. The ensign billowing out on the steam launch is that of the Royal Naval Reserve, and at least two reviewers described the man as a naval officer. Like the Pool itself, naval men were potentially disturbing if not appropriately portrayed. Generally thought to be improvident, drunken, and immoral, sailors were also supposed to resort promiscuously to prostitutes, which not only weakened them individually but threatened Britain as a nation through the long-term degenerative effects of syphilis.[7]

In 1864, in an attempt to improve the supposedly depleted vigor of the Navy, Parliament passed the first of a series of Contagious Diseases Acts, which provoked public controversy until they were repealed in 1886. These aimed at introducing a Parisian-style system of regulation for prostitutes in certain ports where there were a great number of sailors, a plan proponents suggested extending to London. The aim was to lower the incidence of venereal disease in the Navy. The Acts were extremely controversial, and one influential argument against them was openly xenophobic, contending that adopting the custom of registering prostitutes was inappropriate for the English, as it reflected the lewd nature of the French.

In the same spirit some of the reviewers disliked Tissot's picture because it seemed too French: "A clever picture, but hardly nice in its suggestions. More French, shall we say, than English?" wrote one of them, obliquely referring to the questionable sexual morals of the characters.[8] Read in this light, the prominent champagne bottles in the foreground can hardly have been reassuring.

no. 20

21 *Trafalgar Tavern, Greenwich,* 1878
Etching and drypoint, 13⅞ x 9⅞ in.
First state, with clear sky (W. 36, I/II)
Signed and dated in the plate, lower left;
    signed in pencil, lower margin, right;
    red monogram stamp, lower left
Private collection

22 *Trafalgar Tavern, Greenwich,* 1878
Etching and drypoint, 13⅞ x 9¾ in.
Second state, with stormy sky (W. 36, II/II)
Signed and dated in the plate, lower left;
    signed in pencil, lower margin, left;
    red monogram stamp, lower left
Private collection

The tavern is shown from the vantage point of a guest sitting at a table in the dining room, the luxury of which is signaled by a place setting of three glasses, three spoons, and two forks, all as yet untouched. Designed by Joseph Kay in 1837, the Trafalgar was famous for its "whitebait suppers," expensive fish meals unique to London. It also had strong naval associations: its balconies were copies of the stern gallery of *H.M.S. Victory,* Nelson's ship at the Battle of Trafalgar. Significantly, this was also the venue for an annual political event, the Parliamentary fish dinner, a famous occasion for Members of Parliament to indulge themselves in food and drink. The tradition had originated in the eighteenth century and, though temporarily discontinued in 1868, was revived under Disraeli in 1874.[9]

In Tissot's etching, then, the men on the balcony occupy a recognized position of power, a site of government authority, in contrast with the ragged boys literally and figuratively below them. Their top hats, black coats, and casual ease bear witness to their privileged place in society. The boys, on the other hand, are hatless and shoeless, their scrawny legs suggesting poverty and vulnerability. Creeping up the wall of the tavern is a dark stain, which threatens the smooth, blank whiteness of its stone facade; literally intended as algae, it serves as a metaphor for the living conditions of the children, who are probably "mudlarks," familiar London types described by urban ethnographer Henry Mayhew in his *London Labour and the London Poor* (fig. 15). Scavenging the shores at low tide for coal, iron, and copper nails from barges and shipbuilding concerns, these gleaners of society's refuse occupied the bottom of the social hierarchy. One little boy appears to be making a rude gesture at the assembled guests above, although he may be begging or tugging his forelock in

fig. 15. "The Mud-Lark," from Henry Mayhew, *London Labour and the London Poor,* 1862

a gesture of thanks or respect. A series of barriers, including the balcony wall, the cast-iron fence of the terrace, and the high enclosure around Greenwich Hospital, underscore the divisions between the haves and have-nots. In the second state of the print, the ominous sky, carefully rendered to striking effect, suggests that the encounter between the two bodes ill.

How can we explain Tissot's atypical interest in class relations in this work? Perhaps the answer lies partly in his connection to the journalist Thomas Gibson Bowles. In a diary entry of 1874 Bowles describes how he once watched some wealthy diners at a "celebrated inn" at Greenwich throwing coins to three naked boys in the water and attacks the paltriness of a gesture performed "in the fullness of their generosity—or rather in the generosity of their fullness."[10]

no. 21   no. 22

no. 23

City Life

In treating the contemporary cityscape, Tissot addressed concerns similar to those of his former Impressionist allies in France, but while they depicted the streets of Paris, he chose the foreign city of London. The fact that he never sought British citizenship but maintained a distinctly expatriate identity, suggests that he consciously positioned himself as a Frenchman in a strange city, intending perhaps to convey an outsider's perspective on his new surroundings. That Tissot presented his images of London in English art institutions suggests that he was encouraging his audiences to look at their familiar surroundings in a new light, claiming a certain artistic authority in the process; that is, he deliberately chose well-known London locations in order to market the authenticity of his foreign vision. As a visitor, he could literally "see" things the English could not.

A number of his images of the city feature monumental architecture, including buildings in Trafalgar Square and Regent's Park. Before studying painting, Tissot had considered becoming an architect, and he retained an interest in the way architecture shaped both urban experience and his own painterly vision. In these works various architectural elements support and inflect the central narratives, providing clues to the social status and behavior of the figures.

23 *London Visitors*, 1874
   Oil on canvas, 63 x 45 in.
   Signed, lower left
   Exhibited: Royal Academy, 1874
   The Toledo Museum of Art
   Purchased with Funds from the Libbey Endowment
   Gift of Edward Drummond Libbey

London Visitors portrays a group of people in the portico of Britain's National Gallery. At the top of the stairs is a couple, the man engrossed in a book, the woman looking out of the picture and gesturing to the right with her closed umbrella. Coming down the steps toward us is a boy in a long blue coat and yellow stockings, the only note of color in a work dominated by the gray tones of the architecture. Another similarly clad boy in the middle ground accompanies a woman who has her hand on his shoulder. Surrounding the people are the monumental columns of the National Gallery colonnade, echoed by those of the church of St. Martin-in-the-Fields in the background.

When the painting was exhibited at the Royal Academy in 1874, the critics reacted with displeasure. In declaring that "*London Visitors* will not, we fear, add to M. Tissot's reputation," one of them reiterated the uneasy response of many.[1] Why would such an apparently benign image have elicited this outcry? The answers lie in reactions to Tissot's foreign perspective, which took in important, quintessentially British sights of London and altered them in ways that made them seem alien. To begin with, although the picture appears to be a straightforward representation of the site, Tissot actually manipulated the space to suit his artistic purposes. In reality, the colonnade of St. Martin-in-the-Fields is only barely visible from this viewpoint, whereas Tissot has included almost all of it. He chose a recognizable London location, with which his viewers would have been familiar, to unsettle and question their expectations.

The particular view of London before which Tissot's visitors stand, across Trafalgar Square and down Whitehall to the Houses of Parliament, was a famous and recommended perspective on the city from its very center. The boys in the striking blue and yellow costumes were also figures unique to London; they are "bluecoat boys," pupils of Christ's Hospital School, a government-run institution founded in 1553 as a charity for the children of tradesmen. Dating from the sixteenth century, their dress was based on monk's garb and consisted of a blue wool robe with white clerical bands at the neck, woolen knickers, and yellow stockings. Despite continual calls for the modernization of this anachronistic uniform, the faction championing its importance as a picturesque London sight managed to prevent any updating; such quaint relics of the past were reassuring to those unsettled by recent alterations in the social, economic, and physical structures of the city. Proud of its status, the school encouraged spectators to attend its special functions (see fig. 16).

Given the importance of the bluecoat boy to Londoners, his representation was a delicate process. The acceptable way of portraying this character was as the chubby-cheeked, humble lad of the *Graphic* illustration; art critics disliked Tissot's departure from this template, and several expressed disapproval of "the ugliness and awkwardness of the bluecoat boy."[2] The boys in the painting are indeed thin, pale, and ungainly, their lips parted in slack-jawed expressions. Perhaps this rendering reminded viewers uncomfortably of some rumors concerning the school, the "secret vice" darkly hinted at in a letter to *The Times* in 1867.[3] Rather than being wholesome symbols of London and English identity, then, Tissot's bluecoat boys potentially harbored vicious tendencies.

Another troubling aspect of the work is suggested by a reviewer's remark that the woman's face bore "an unpleasing sneer" and that her actions were "inexplicable."[4] The figure of the outward-gazing woman was charged for its contemporary viewers in a manner we can only faintly reconstitute by reading about recommended behavior for ladies. Dictated by the proliferating etiquette books of the time, the correct,

fig. 16. "Public Supper at Christ's Hospital," cover of the *Graphic*, April 9, 1870

carded cigar in the foreground, suggests that the prescribed viewer of the canvas is male. Its presence invests the space in front of the picture with bourgeois masculinity, for the cigar was the preferred tobacco product of the upper- and upper-middle-class gentleman in both Britain and France. Attesting to his wealth in disposing of a practically unsmoked and valuable object, the off-screen man has cast it aside upon encountering a lady in public, as was proper. The fact that Tissot removed the cigar and shifted the woman's gaze off to the right in his later, smaller version of this composition (c. 1874; Milwaukee Art Center) suggests that he himself was uncomfortable with so unambiguously suggesting the recipient of the woman's glance.

If Tissot's lady is looking at a man, her reasons for doing so are obscure, and this lack of clarity triggered yet more unease. In the nineteenth-century city moral anxiety over prostitutes successfully masquerading as chaste women contributed to a fear that a woman's stare could be an irresistible snare. The ambiguity of the woman's actual intentions was the operative aspect of this sort of charged encounter, with the man left wondering about the gazer's sexual availability. The viewer of the picture was overdetermined as a modern, bourgeois man, but only if he was enough of one to understand—and condone—this inside joke. Others were puzzled and threatened, left out of the exchange. Not surprisingly, one critic wrote of the figures: "though we admit them to be English, they are so rather as seen from the French than from the English point of view."[6]

YALE ONLY

ladylike mien in public was a demurely downcast glance; a woman was expected to avoid calling attention to herself by dressing gaudily or, particularly, by staring. In the words of one social commentator, "a pleasing modest reserve, and retiring delicacy, that avoids the vulgar stare of the public eye, and blushing, withdraws from the gaze of admiration, is beyond all doubt one of the principal beauties of the female character."[5]

The lady in *London Visitors* does not cleave to the prescribed female gaze of self-effacement; ignoring the dictates of etiquette, she returns our look directly, in a stare which goes unnoticed by her male protector. Left out of this central narrative, her male companion loses himself in the contemplation of history and culture, while the woman is free to engage the viewer in the distinctly modern, urban interplay of a gaze between strangers.

Most importantly, not only does the woman look, she clearly looks at a man. A key passage in the picture, the dis-

no. 24

24 *The Portico of the National Gallery, London*, 1878
      Etching and drypoint, 14⅞ x 8¼ in. (W. 40)
      Signed and dated in the plate, lower right; signed in pencil,
        lower margin, left; red monogram stamp, lower margin, right
      Private collection

Tissot returned to the site of *London Visitors* (no. 23) for this more informal etching, which, unusually for him, is not a direct copy from any known painting. It portrays a similar tourist couple on the steps, but the bluecoat boy has been replaced by a young woman carrying an artist's portfolio under her arm. Significantly, the boldly staring woman of *London Visitors* has become a discreetly veiled lady meekly attending to her male companion.

Presumably the woman in the foreground, modeled by Kathleen Newton (see nos. 54–62), has been pursuing her artistic education (or merely a hobby) by sketching after the Old Master paintings in the National Gallery. It was widely held that copying works of art was a suitable occupation for a woman. Many young ladies learned drawing as an accomplishment to make them more appealing as potential wives, but few went on to study art seriously. Women were supposed to have unique abilities as copyists, a belief some Victorian theorists connected with the fact that they were biologically designed literally to reproduce. Men, on the other hand, produced, and creativity was considered a male trait.

The clarity of line in this print, most noticeable on the church in the background and on the crisply outlined columns, demonstrates Tissot's ability to etch in as finely detailed a style as he painted. In a mysterious touch he seems to have enlarged Newton's shadow quite implausibly, given that it lies to the right of her when the light source is clearly on the same side. The looming bulk almost suggests the presence of another person—perhaps the artist himself, unable to resist hinting at his own presence with his lover on this artistic pilgrimage.

25 *The Warrior's Daughter*
also known as *The Convalescent*, c. 1878
Oil on panel, 14¼ x 8⅝ in.
Signed, lower right
Manchester City Art Galleries

Like *London Visitors* (no. 23), *The Warrior's Daughter* portrays a covert visual exchange between a young, attractive woman and the viewer. Set in Cumberland Terrace in Regent's Park, London, the work depicts an elderly gentleman in a bath chair pushed by a younger, drably dressed man, probably a servant. Accompanying them on the outing is a young woman in a green plaid dress and a fur mantle, clutching a matching muff and gazing out of the picture. Behind them is an iron fence and the elaborate facades of two buildings divided by a freestanding archway.

The old "warrior" is presumably a veteran who received his injury fighting for his country. Much like the gentleman consulting the guidebook in *London Visitors*, he is oblivious to the individual who has caught his daughter's attention. Contemporaries picked up on the fact that the woman was engaged in illicit gazing, and one reviewer described the man as "attended by a young lady, who evidently is not always under her father's eye."[7] Her outward gaze, like that of the woman in *London Visitors*, was read as part of a system of looks to which the male chaperone is not privy.

The age difference between the two main figures in *The Warrior's Daughter* signaled that the fashionable, modern young lady was escaping control of the now-ineffectual older generation, a notion emphasized by the background architecture. Designed by John Nash in 1826, Cumberland Terrace was one of most elaborate sections of the Regent's Park development; it was decorated with allegorical, white stucco sculptures of the arts, trades, and sciences surrounding the figure of Britannia, one of which is just visible through the tree branches in *The Warrior's Daughter*. Originally an architectural embodiment of the grandeur of Britain, the elaborate structures of Regent's Park had come to exemplify for Victorians the false taste of the previous era. One writer termed the "ugly terraces" the "worst follies of the Grecian architectural mania which disgraced the beginning of this century."[8] As such, they represented the old man's generation, young when the buildings were first erected but now visibly weakened and faded in authority. Indeed his hat and coat are the same color as the facades, while the young woman's outfit rhymes in color with the young green grass of the lawn. Representative of the vigorous present, the young woman with her secret communication rebels against the sham authority of the past, symbolized by the tawdry imitations of classical sculpture.

no. 25

26 *The Organ Grinder*, 1878
    Etching and drypoint, 10¼ x 6½ in. (W. 38)
    Signed and dated in the plate, lower left
    Private collection

Though set in the same London location as *The Warrior's Daughter* (no. 25), Regent's Park, *The Organ Grinder* represents an extremely different use of the space. The etching is unique in Tissot's œuvre in its focus on a single, male, working-class figure. In contrast to the graceful curves and symmetrical, repetitive elements of the architecture, the wizened organ grinder slumps under the burden of his instrument, a haphazard bundle of darkly cross-hatched, wrinkled clothing without a visible identity.

The organ grinder was not a skilled laborer or artisan; he turned a crank to make a machine produce music and depended on public charity in modern London's "theater of the streets." Many organ grinders were Italian immigrants seeking work. Tissot emphasizes the pathetic nature of the vignette in the hopeful tilt of the old man's hat brim toward the open window, and in the poised expectation of the monkey waiting to clash its cymbals. The dark square of the opening indicates that the music has successfully penetrated to his audience, but no appreciation, either financial or aesthetic, seems forthcoming.

Tissot's countryman Gustave Doré had portrayed an organ grinder in the influential travelogue *London: A Pilgrimage* (fig. 17), with accompanying text by Blanchard Jerrold describing the pleasure the audience received from the music.[9] Doré's and Tissot's images have little in common, however: the former depicts the organ grinder entertaining ragged, solemn-faced urchins in East London; in the Tissot he is in no such "appropriate" place, having ventured into the bourgeois neighborhood of Regent's Park, where he lacks any apparent audience beyond an open window.

Interestingly, in the decade before Tissot arrived in London, the presence of the organ grinder in such neighborhoods had been the subject of a controversy formulated along class lines. In 1864 Michael Bass, Member of Parliament, had introduced a petition into the House of Commons regarding street music. Under the law as it stood, policemen could move street musicians on if they were playing in a thoroughfare or "near a house," but gardens, alleys, and mews were exempt from this rule. Arguing that only the upper classes could afford the sort of "sentimental conservatism" that condoned street music, because their houses were set well back from the road, Bass painted a picture of the middle classes as under siege, by organ grinders in particular. Those who needed to work out of their homes were the most annoyed, and a number of well-known artists and musicians signed the petition for reforming the law.[10] Bass attempted to convince his readers that the organ grinders were dirty, foreign, and dangerous, destroying the quality of life of the English city. Terming them "fiends," he accused them of assaulting females and warned that "Italians are generally persons of very bad character and most immoral habits."[11] Playing on xenophobia and sexual anxieties, Bass ultimately had a bill passed which partly realized his goals.

Perhaps as a fellow foreigner and something of an outsider himself, Tissot identified with the organ grinder; after all, both were dependent on the willingness of strangers to pay for the products of their labor. Tissot had ceased to exhibit at the Royal Academy in 1876, and by this point in his career was apparently somewhat ostracized from polite society for living with his model and mistress Kathleen Newton. Possibly he felt that the same respectable middle-class artists and writers who had signed the petition against organ grinders were now arrayed against him, believing him to be a foreign source of corruption and a mere hack.[12] If Tissot did think of the organ grinder as an alter ego, it was probably in a humorous way, however, since he was financially successful and had his own circle of friends and fellow artists.

no. 26

fig. 17. Gustave Doré, "The Organ in the Court,"
from *London: A Pilgrimage*, 1872

no. 27

On Shipboard

Born in the port city of Nantes, Tissot retained what must have been an early fascination for ships throughout his career. From the early 1860s in France he had skillfully depicted the intricacies of rigging, both modern and historic, demonstrating an impressively accurate knowledge of lines and sails. Transposed to the island nation of Britain, his interest in shipping took on new meanings. Brought up with the notion that, as the song goes, "Britannia rules the waves," English audiences were more acutely focused on—and appreciative of—representations of maritime subjects.

Most extensively, Tissot used ships as the context for scenes of courtship. Like the river-craft in the pictures set on the Thames (see nos. 18–20), ships had symbolic associations with romance. Popular works of his early period in England, such as *Boarding the Yacht* (fig. 4), represent naval men at leisure dallying with pretty young ladies. In this regard his ships resemble the craft described by his friend Thomas Gibson Bowles: "we little coasting yachts, who only pretend to go to sea, and who are never really happy till we are tied to the side of a quay, with a blue or white ensign flying and a party of ladies on board at lunch, are the most arrant impostors perhaps in England."[1] Like Bowles, Tissot seems to have preferred to be safely at anchor in sight of land rather than on the open ocean.

The function of Tissot's shipboard settings shifted during his sojourn in England. Originally they served mainly as backdrops for scenes of courtship and entertainment, but by 1880 the scenarios had become more serious, including leave-taking and emigration.

27   *The Ball on Shipboard*, c. 1874
   Oil on canvas, 33⅛ x 51 in.
   Signed, lower right
   Exhibited: Royal Academy, 1874
   Tate Gallery, London
   Presented by the Trustees of the Chantrey Bequest, 1937

In this elaborate, somewhat hard-to-decipher composition, a group of men and women relax at an afternoon dance on board a ship decorated in "full dress," with all the flags in its collection draped on the rigging. When the picture was exhibited at the Royal Academy in 1874, reviewers identified its setting as a man-of-war off Cowes on the Isle of Wight. The prestigious and elite Royal Yacht Club at Cowes held a yearly regatta at which, Tissot informed the Impressionist painter Berthe Morisot, was to be found the most fashionable society in England.[2]

The flags create a riot of saturated colors; in the words of one critic, the canvas "looks as if it had fallen against a damp rainbow."[3] Closest to the viewer in the right foreground is the Union flag; on the ceiling, from front to back, are the Royal Standard of Queen Victoria and the flags of the German Navy, the Austrian Empire, France, and the United States. To the left a retired captain places his hand protectively on the back of a young woman's chair; she gazes past him expectantly. The pointing parasol in the empty chair next to her guides our eye to two women wearing identical white dresses with navy trim; they are accompanied by a drowsy elderly chaperone, who at first appears to be sporting a knot of ribbons on his boater (a closer examination reveals a visual pun—the bow belongs to a woman behind him). In the distance uniformed seamen are standing and watching the couples dancing on a lower deck. Behind the ranks sit several more men, their bare feet plainly visible; with them, at the very end of the distant vignette, are two scarlet-coated military officers, one of them standing with a gun.

The trajectory of the viewer's sight moves from a female-dominated space, characterized by expectant stillness, parasols, ruffles, and bouquets, to an area in which men and women are present in equal numbers, matched up in the vigorous activity of the dance, to the exclusively male world of the Navy, ending in the reminder of potential military force in the shape of the man with the gun. In the familiar image of the "ship of state," the ship is a microcosm of society or government; this particular ship, moreover, was a weapon of war. The picture suggests that beneath the superficial layer of social elegance lie the firm wooden planks and brass railings—and military power—of imperial Britain, an idea underlined by the British flag hanging closest to our viewpoint. The guests enjoy themselves in happy ignorance of the political overtones of their environment: to this segment of society, socializing and dancing are of more immediate concern.

Tissot may have intended to portray the cream of English society, but the negative public reaction to his picture indicates that he failed. Increasingly critics called the social world he described in his works "vulgar," a complicated, charged term at this time. The Victorian sage John Ruskin, one of those who used this word, defined vulgarity as the opposite of "gentlemanliness." It involved a pretension to what one was not: "An undue regard to appearances and manners …and an assumption of behaviour, language, or dress, unsuited to them, by persons in inferior stations of life."[4]

The label "vulgar" suggested social superiority on the part of the person using it, and in the case of *The Ball on Shipboard* it was intended to alert viewers to the fact that women at the ball were not actually of the class to which they aspired. "The girls who are spread about in every attitude are evidently the 'high life below stairs' of the port, who have borrowed their mistresses' dresses for the nonce," chided one reviewer.[5] One of the most obvious triggers for such remarks was the unseemly display of décolletage in the grouping in the mid-distant left: the women in the green and blue dresses are apparently revealing too much flesh for daylight hours.[6]

As viewers looked for signs of the social identity of Tissot's characters, the ladies' costumes may have been the major source of anxiety. In times past most members of upper-class British society had known (or at least known of) one another, and their financial status was assumed. Now the newly wealthy industrial magnates needed to display their financial qualifications for entering the best circles, which they did by dressing their wives and daughters in the most expensive and showy gowns available. The more ostentatious costumes of the day were regarded with suspicion, therefore, as indications of attempted social climbing. Tissot's elaborately ruffled and flounced women caused uneasiness because they reminded viewers too strongly of the frightening instability of modern society, in which the nouveau riche could force their way into any gathering on the basis of their wealth alone.

In *The Ball on Shipboard* several of the women are wearing identical dresses, an unusual pictorial device but one which Tissot often favored ("spot the dress" is a rewarding game to play in his œuvre). In the group in the left background, two women sport identical sea-green outfits, two light blue. Three ladies wear pink dresses with maroon trim. Most noticeable of all are the two in the center of the picture in the same white-and-blue gown and straw boater. In a world that was in flux and all but illegible, the appearance of replicas must have been highly disturbing, preventing identification of class or character altogether.

If Tissot sought to prove his own social status by depicting a fashionable event in high society, his attempt failed; like the ladies in their low-necked gowns, he seems to have appeared as a vulgar person trying to deceive others as to the nobility of his birth and moral character.

28 *The Gallery of H. M. S. Calcutta*, c. 1876

> Oil on canvas, 25⅞ x 36¼ in.
> Signed, lower left
> Exhibited: Grosvenor Gallery, 1877
> Tate Gallery, London. Presented by Samuel Courtauld, 1936

In this gracefully composed picture, a young officer and two well-dressed women stand by the rails of a secluded corner of a man-of-war, perhaps sitting out a dance during a ball. Like many other Tissot images, including *Boarding the Yacht* (fig. 4), *The Thames* (no. 20), *How Happy I Could Be with Either* (no. 35), and *Holyday* (no. 45), the work focuses on two women and a man, suggesting but not specifying the relationships between them.

As a reviewer noted, "perhaps it is the artist's whim thus to set his admirers puzzling their brains as to the occult meaning of his productions, when in reality there is no such object in his thoughts, which were wholly occupied with the conception of a new artistic effect."[7] Like Whistler and the artists of the Aesthetic Movement, Tissot was certainly interested in producing objects of contemplation and beauty without immediate narrative content. Intricately tied together through subtle color harmonies and curving lines, with the hourglass pattern on the wrought-iron decorative railings rhyming with the figure of the woman on the right, the work illustrates Tissot's skill in creating a unified composition. "We would direct our readers' attention to the painting of the flesh seen through the thin white muslin dresses," wrote one admiring critic; "manual dexterity could hardly achieve a greater triumph."[8]

Yet Tissot included so many apparently meaningful details that trying to determine his "occult meaning" is irresistible. Given the way the chair hugs the flounces on her skirt, and the fact that she is pinned between two chairs, the lady in the exquisite white muslin dress with the yellow ribbons appears to have been recently sitting with the woman in blue; perhaps she has sprung up in consternation at the turn the conversation has taken. Likewise, the other young lady pulls discontentedly back from the railing, which forms possibly symbolic heart shapes. Although the delicately rendered reflection in the background pairs the man with this woman, he looks intently at the other as she covers her cheek with a fan. To those familiar with the Victorian "language of the fan," covering the left ear with an open fan meant "do not betray our secret."[9] Whether or not Tissot intended that meaning here, he was certainly intrigued by the infinite number of uses for this decorative accessory (see no. 40). The possible readings of the characters' relationships become yet more complex when we notice that the young sailor has a ring on his wedding finger. Unlike *The Ball on Shipboard*, with its gay background of yachts at a regatta, the picture depicts the soot and grime of the modern Portsmouth dockyards, and the gray sky contributes to the oppressive, puzzling sense of tension between the characters.

Designed by Sir Robert Sepping and built in Bombay, *H.M.S. Calcutta* had been launched in 1831. It saw a great deal of service, in the Baltic during the Crimean War in 1855 and again in the Second China War of 1856–58. In 1877 it was retired to become an experimental gunnery ship in Portsmouth. But perhaps Tissot's choice of this vessel had more to do with its name than its history; given the emphasis on the female form, Malcolm Warner has suggested that the title could be a sly reference to the French pun *quel cul tu as* (what an ass you have). In the background are two-decker ships used as accommodation for crews, while the vessel to the left is an Indian troop ship.[10]

no. 29

29–34 *The Gallery of H.M.S. Calcutta,* 1876
Drypoint (W. 25)

29 Trial proof, largely outlines, 10⅜ x 14 in.
Private collection

30 Trial proof of right side, 7⅞ x 6½ in. (image)
Private collection

31 Trial proof of right side, 7 x 5⅞ in. (image)
Private collection

32 Trial proof of right side, 7⁷⁄₁₆ x 5¾ in. (image)
Private collection

33 *Bon à tirer* proof, 10⁵⁄₁₆ x 14⅛ in.
Signed and dated in the plate, upper right;
inscribed in pencil: "Bon a Tirer," lower margin
Private collection

34 Impression from the published edition, 10⁵⁄₁₆ x 14³⁄₁₆ in.
Signed and dated in the plate, upper right;
red monogram stamp, lower right
Private collection

Tissot made this drypoint after his own painting of the same title (no. 28), reproducing the image precisely with the exception of the removal of the sailors in the rowboat below. In an unusual move he also granted permission for an engraving to appear in the *Graphic,* under the title *Souvenir of a Ball on Shipboard.*[11] By allowing the reproduction of his painting on a popular level, while also producing an upscale drypoint version for the higher-end market, he maximized both his exposure and his profits.

The succession of trial proofs (nos. 29–32) show Tissot first outlining the design, then working up the right side, in particular the crucial figure of the woman with the fan. The *bon à tirer* (no. 33) was the proof the artist gave his printer to use as a prototype and to follow as closely as possible in the print as published (no. 34).

no. 30

no. 33

no. 31

no. 34

no. 32

35 *How Happy I Could Be with Either*, 1877
Etching and drypoint, 9⁹⁄₁₆ x 14 in. (W. 30)
Signed and dated in the plate, lower right
Private collection

Perhaps in response to negative criticism of his painting *The Thames* (no. 20) when it was shown at the Royal Academy exhibition of 1876—pointedly trying to give the English public what it wanted—Tissot reworked basically the same composition as *Portsmouth Dockyard* (Tate Gallery), which he exhibited at the Grosvenor Gallery in 1877 to more favorable response. He created the present etching after that painting. Its title is from an air in John Gay's *The Beggar's Opera* (1728): "How happy could I be with either, / Were t'other dear charmer away!"

Examining the differences between the two images highlights what was disturbingly unconventional about *The Thames*. Both contain a man and two women in the stern of a boat, the front end of which disappears into the foreground. But the present work shows them traversing the clear water of Portsmouth harbor rather than the muddy water of the Thames, in an old-fashioned rowboat rather than a modern steam launch. Here the man wears the uniform of a prominent regiment, the 42nd Royal Highlanders (or Black Watch) which, unlike the Navy, had a secure reputation for courage and discipline. In the background are two decommissioned warships and a crew of sailors neatly rowing in unison, inspiring confidence in the discipline of the British Navy. The clarity of the work's composition echoes the legibility of its meaning: the man and women do not overlap as they do in *The Thames* but stand out distinctly from one another, their faces plainly visible.

Whereas in *The Thames* the man's intentions and the meaning of the image are ambiguous, here Tissot sets up a clearly comic situation. The Highland sergeant turns away from a disconsolate-looking companion toward the woman who is obviously speaking to him, illustrating the old story of the man trying to choose between two women. In the background the double figureheads, clothed rather than bare-breasted as in *The Thames*, humorously mirror the two rivals for the Highlander's attention. Despite the indecision suggested by the title, the man seems to favor one of the two, a theme common in both French and English art. Not surprisingly, while Tissot does not appear to have shown the etching of *The Thames* after its first appearance, impressions of the present print appeared frequently in exhibitions.

Given its prominence in his work, Tissot's favorite theme of one man accompanied by two women may have carried personal meaning. Perhaps, like the novelist George Meredith in *Beauchamp's Career* (1876), he intended his two female leads to represent the countries between which he was torn, France and England.[12]

no. 35

36 *Emigrants*, 1880
    Etching and drypoint, 13⅝ x 6⁵⁄₁₆ in. (W. 45)
    Signed in the plate, lower left; signed in pencil, lower margin, left;
        red monogram stamp, lower margin, right
    Private collection

Against a confusing background of criss-crossing masts and
rigging, a young mother is about to take the symbolic first
step onto the ship that will carry her to a new and unknown
country. With one arm she carries both a child and a bundle
of goods; with the other she steadies herself on the rail. The
man helping her onto the ship may be her husband or
another male relative. Behind her is an elderly man and a
young child, representing the universality of the drive to
leave one's home in search of a better life.

    Tissot deftly creates a sense of depth by means of the spar
in the foreground that recedes from the upper right to the
middle distance. The subtle touches in the sky convincingly
create a sense of foreboding, as do the messily coiled ropes,
which suggest a lack of safety, care, and industriousness on
the part of the crew. Conditions on emigrant liners were
often poor; tiny cabins, rough seas, candle-lighting, bad food,
and filthy accommodations were not unusual. Confusion and
poor treatment at both ends of the journey often added to
the difficulties faced by families like those depicted here.

no. 36

37 *Goodbye (On the Mersey)*, c. 1881
    Oil on canvas, 33 x 21 in.
    Signed, lower right
    Exhibited: Royal Academy, 1881
    The Forbes Magazine Collection, New York

Under threatening gray skies an ocean liner departs from
the port of Liverpool via the river Mersey, while friends and
relatives of the passengers wave hats and handkerchiefs in
farewell. As viewers, we are in the position of those staying
behind, standing on a small local ferry. Identifiable by its
black-tipped red funnels, the enormous steamer leaving the
harbor is from the most successful of the Liverpool passenger
services, the Cunard Line, which sailed to New York. From
the time the first regular steamship services from Liverpool
to North America began in the 1840s, with sail almost fully
giving way to steam by the 1860s, Liverpool's shipbuilding
industry had flourished. The new ironclad liners made ocean
travel safer, faster, more predictable (a trip to the United
States took about ten days), and cheaper. As economic hard-
ships at home drove more and more people to seek new lives
abroad, Liverpool became the major port of embarkation for
European and British emigrants; record numbers left for the
U. S. in the very year Tissot painted this work.[13]

Charles Dickens described the departure of a ferry such
as this one, noting the complex feelings the great oceangoing
ships evoked: "Knots of people stood on the wharf, gazing
with a kind of 'dread delight' on the far-famed American
steamer."[14] Steamers and emigration did indeed provoke
mixed emotions, offering hope and adventure but also fear
of the unknown. Tissot's somber palette of black, white, and
shades of brown suggests anxiety or solemnity, and bizarre
details enhance our sense of discomfort: the little girl all
in black on the right appears peculiarly headless, her hair
streaming out from under her father's tight grip.

Both of the women raising their handkerchiefs in the
foreground have the features of Tissot's mistress Kathleen
Newton (see nos. 54–62). After 1878 she seems to have been
his only young adult female model, an oddly obsessive
limitation for an artist and particularly for a realist. Given
this fact and his need to paint from life, presumably he was
forced to replicate her as many times as his composition
demanded. This does not fully explain his choice to paint
Newton exclusively, however—nor his strange fondness for
doubling, which indeed he practiced even when he had many
models available; he painted apparently identical women in
The Ball on Shipboard (no. 27), for example. He seems to have
seen no problem with the decidedly unrealistic image of two
or three clones of the same woman together, sometimes even
drawing attention to it, as here, by clothing them similarly.
Perhaps painting replicas of his female models metaphorically enacted Tissot's own attempt to replicate the appearance of the world through his mimetic, realist technique. His
clones are both symbols and illustrations of his ability to
reproduce reality.

YALE ONLY

no. 37

38 *Two Friends*, 1882

Etching and drypoint, 23¼ x 10¼ in. (W. 55)
Impression with hand-colored flags in title margin
Signed and dated in the plate, lower right; red monogram stamp, lower right
Private collection

Tissot was preoccupied with images of leave-taking at this time, perhaps because he himself was contemplating a return to Paris. In *Emigrants* (no. 36), *Goodbye (On the Mersey)* (no. 37), and other works, he explored the theme of travel and escape, despite—or perhaps because of—the fact that this period is commonly said to have been his most reclusive, as he withdrew into the happy, if not respectable, domestic circle of Kathleen Newton and her children. Newton appears in some of these pictures, and they form a distinct contrast to the calm green world of the garden images (see nos. 56, 59–61). As he does appear to have traveled with Newton to various destinations, including Paris, the images may in part record actual journeys, but the sheer number of them suggests that they were more than a mere travelogue. It is as if Tissot, perhaps somewhat unwelcome in respectable social circles, were expressing his desire to escape with Newton— not to arrive, but simply to be in transit where their respective reputations were meaningless to passing strangers.

The man clinging to the rigging to grasp the hand of his friend in one last farewell looks strikingly like Tissot's Prodigal Son (see nos. 72–75) as well as his portrait of the English spiritualist William Eglinton (fig. 18). Eglinton did travel to the United States in February 1881, which may have suggested to Tissot the idea of using him as a model. Newton modeled for the two women to the left.

The smiles of the ladies and the excitement of the man on the left waving his hand make the mood of the etching more jubilant than somber. Given Tissot's interest in the American market for his prints, perhaps he intended to affirm the renewed friendship between England and the United States. The word "Alabama" on the bundle in the foreground would have triggered associations with a notoriously low point in

fig. 18. James Tissot, *William Eglinton*, 1885, etching, 6¼ x 4 in. (W. 84)
Art Gallery of Ontario, Toronto, Gift of Allan and Sondra Gotlieb, 1994

Anglo-American relations. During the American Civil War the British allowed the South to commission a warship, the *Alabama*, from a shipbuilder in Liverpool. It caused considerable damage to the Union Navy, and after the conflict the States charged Great Britain with "veiled hostility" and "insincere neutrality" in a well-publicized, controversial case that was not settled until 1872. By the time of Tissot's etching, however, tensions between the two countries had resolved into amicable relations.

no. 38

no. 39

Social Graces

The scenes of festive events and crowds at fashionable gatherings that Tissot painted and etched during his London years served a double purpose. First, they allowed him to explore the ways of contemporary life among the bourgeoisie, in favor of which he entirely abandoned his interest in historical subjects. Second, and perhaps more urgently, they helped to situate him as a respectable member of the very stratum of society he depicted.

Tissot insinuated himself into the elite classes of England very quickly. By 1873 he had become financially secure enough to purchase an expensive villa in St. John's Wood, in which he entertained lavishly.[1] In September 1871 his friend Degas wrote from Paris: "Tissot, why the devil do you not send me a line? They tell me you are earning a lot of money. Do give me some figures…give me some idea how I could profit from England." On February 18, 1873, he exclaimed, "you are getting on like a house on fire! 900 pounds—but that's a fortune!" adding enviously, "I hear that you have bought a house—my mouth is still open."[2] There is a great deal of evidence to support the idea that Tissot had prodigious skill as a self-marketer. He gradually found exhibition venues and dealers not only in London, but also in the northern industrial cities of Newcastle, Manchester, Liverpool, Leeds, and Glasgow. In a letter of 1879, in his quaint English, he asked a potential purchaser of his etching *October* (no. 50) to recommend "the best of the picture dealer in Newcastle," who could "show all my etchings or anything else in this town."[3]

Tissot was in need of more than just critical and financial success in London; his reputation as a respectable individual was also at stake. Artists were of dubious social status as self-made men who had to work for a living. But Tissot faced obstacles other than his profession. According to his first biographer, George Bastard, his first years in England were marked by the suspicion that he was a political exile, and his name was not officially cleared of associations with the Paris Commune until some time in 1874. The Commune, a short-lived left-wing government of the city in the wake of the Franco-Prussian War, was composed of a politically heterogeneous mixture of groups, mostly from the lower-middle and working classes. The Parisian National Guard, of which Tissot was a member, was a prominent force in the establishment of the Commune, but the degree of his actual involvement is still a matter of debate. The fact remains that he does seem to have had reason to flee his luxurious Parisian home.[4]

Given the position Tissot was attempting to negotiate in English society, perhaps his pictures from this period also represented his desire to placate his new audiences and declare his allegiance to them. His pictures of balls and people enjoying fashionable seaside towns indicated that he himself had "arrived," literally and metaphorically, and that he recognized the codes and norms of the society in which he found himself. He seems by nature to have been fascinated with etiquette, interior decor, and elegant accessories such as ladies' fans; raised in a port town, the son of a linen draper, he would also have been fearful of exposing his lack of "breeding" through a social faux pas. Getting the details right was important for artist and socialite alike.

Tissot's pictures of English social ritual frequently provoked criticism, however. One critic dismissed *Hush!* as "but a sketch—not much nearer completion than a Du Maurier in *Punch*."[5] This oft-repeated sentiment was more than a humorous dig; it actually pointed to one of the novel aspects of Tissot's painting. Like George Du Maurier's cartoons, such as "Gentle Overtures Towards Friendship" (fig. 19), Tissot's works depict the everyday life of society in a detailed, sharply focused, linear style. No central activity takes priority; the all-over technique, like Du Maurier's, suggests the way the image is meant to be read, in a slow pan from incident to incident. Again like a periodical illustrator, Tissot seeks to capture a wide range of recognizable London types, from the beautiful young lady demurely flirting to the stock figure of the buxom, middle-aged woman who inappropriately displays her arms and bosom and ogles the crowd through a lorgnette.

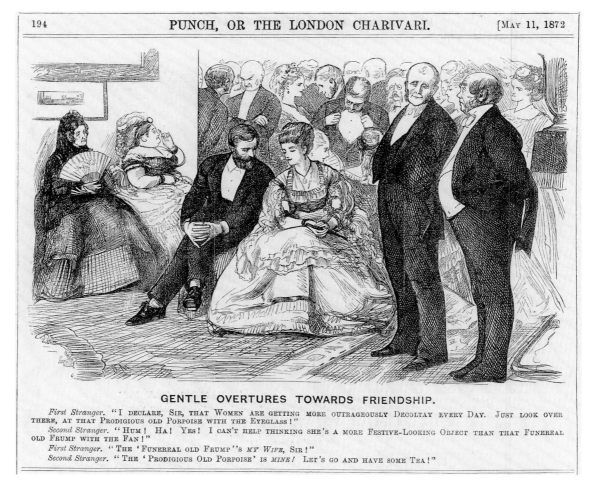

GENTLE OVERTURES TOWARDS FRIENDSHIP.

First Stranger. "I DECLARE, SIR, THAT WOMEN ARE GETTING MORE OUTRAGEOUSLY DECOLTAY EVERY DAY. JUST LOOK OVER THERE, AT THAT PRODIGIOUS OLD PORPOISE WITH THE EYEGLASS!"

Second Stranger. "HUM! HA! YES! I CAN'T HELP THINKING SHE'S A MORE FESTIVE-LOOKING OBJECT THAN THAT FUNEREAL OLD FRUMP WITH THE FAN!"

First Stranger. "THE 'FUNEREAL OLD FRUMP''S *MY WIFE,* SIR!"

Second Stranger. "THE 'PRODIGIOUS OLD PORPOISE' IS *MINE!* LET'S GO AND HAVE SOME TEA!"

fig. 19. George Du Maurier, "Gentle Overtures Towards Friendship," *Punch*, May 11, 1872

In this cultivation of affinities to images of popular culture such as magazine illustrations—or, in other cases, photographs and fashion plates—Tissot demonstrated his adherence to Charles Baudelaire's famous dictum that artists should embrace "the fugitive, fleeting beauty of present-day life, the distinguishing character of that quality…we have called 'modernity.'" Baudelaire believed that modern beauty could be discovered not just in the contemporary environment itself, but also in mass-produced representations of it. He acknowledged the special aesthetic qualities of fashion plates, colored engravings, and lithography.[6] Subscribing to Baudelaire's aesthetic philosophy, Tissot deliberately created works that resembled these popular art forms.

39 *Hush!*, c. 1874–75
Oil on canvas, 29 x 44 in.
Signed, lower right
Exhibited: Royal Academy, 1875
Manchester City Art Galleries

This scene at an upper-class social event, in which elegant men and women gather around a young lady about to perform on a violin, was one of Tissot's greatest commercial successes, purchased by the dealer Agnew's for 1200 guineas.[7] Recognized as a salon in Kensington, the drawing room dominates the upper half of the picture, with its swags of gold drapery, plaster moldings, floral displays, gilt-framed mirrors, and glaring gas chandeliers, while the lower part is full of gaily-dressed ladies in elaborately ruffled gowns, attended by men in formal black-and-white evening dress. Following the sweep of the staircase and the deep curve of the wall of the room, the guests flood into the space in an arc from the left, creating a literal "social circle." On the right are two Indian princes, dressed in royal costume. Their inclusion may reflect Tissot's own interest in India, of which there is evidence in a letter he wrote about the sale of a book of Indian paintings.[8]

Since the first appearance of this work, reviewers have attempted to identify portraits in the crowd. One writer identified the violinist as Madame Castellan, the pianist as Jules Benedict, and other guests as Diaz de Soria and Sir Arthur Sullivan, the composer.[9] More plausibly one can recognize Tissot's artist friends Giuseppe de Nittis and Ferdinand Heilbuth in the doorway, and Thomas Gibson Bowles talking to the lady in the blue dress in the foreground. By portraying this particular social set and including his close friends, Tissot created a world much like that of Gustave Courbet's *Studio of the Painter* (1855; Musée d'Orsay), in which he was not only at home but secure in his support.

The presence of Bowles, publisher of *Vanity Fair*, reminded the viewer of the fact that Tissot had contributed caricatures to this popular magazine; such an affiliation would have provided him an entrée into the highest social circles. One of the reasons for the periodical's success, after all, was its aura of the insider's perspective, which rendered its caricatures more amusing than if they had been produced by some anti-Establishment publication.[10] Bowles had commissioned humorous sketches of various characters in the Second Empire when Tissot was still resident in Paris, and the young artist turned out some surprisingly vicious caricatures, including one of Napoleon III himself (fig. 1).

If Tissot belonged in this group, he encouraged his viewers to feel that they did too by including obvious examples of those who did not. Like *Too Early* (fig. 3), in which embarrassed guests attempt to make the best of the fact that they have arrived at a ball before the appropriate time, *Hush!* contains outsider figures who functioned to make the painting's first viewers at the Royal Academy feel superior. Reviewers frequently drew attention to the fact that the Indian princes were ill at ease in their surroundings; like the premature guests in *Too Early*, they are misfits in this social environment. Staring at a young, fair woman whose body is exposed by the plunging neckline of her evening gown, the princes were described by one reviewer as "ogling Orientals …ready to devour a young lady violinist."[11] Such a scene of a dark-skinned man looking with apparent desire at a white-skinned woman was potentially disturbing to Victorian viewers conditioned by racist rhetoric, but Tissot defuses it by making the Indians the objects of a joke.

no. 40

40 *The Fan*, c. 1875
    Oil on canvas, 15¼ x 20½ in.
    Signed, lower left
    Wadsworth Atheneum, Hartford, Connecticut
    The Ella Gallup Sumner and Mary Catlin Sumner Collection

A young woman flutters a fan over her forehead in coquettish reaction to an unseen speaker. She sits with her arms resting against the back of an armchair draped in a Japanese embroidery, the ruffles of her sleeves echoing the multiple folds of the fan. Oddly compressed, the background with the potted plant to the left and the palm fronds of Tissot's conservatory to the right becomes a flat screen against which the woman's delicate, lively profile stands out. Tissot was fascinated by the fan as a uniquely feminine attribute; he frequently portrayed women in characteristic gestures with these objects. Indeed, like his friends Degas and de Nittis, he even painted fan decorations; one example shows blue cupid figures sporting around a modern nymph and satyr (fig. 20).

Clearly Tissot understood the role of the fan in courtship. As the English essayist Joseph Addison remarked in an oft-quoted line, "women are armed with fans as men with swords, and sometimes do more execution with them."[12] This coyly wielded instrument of flirtation could intimate what a respectable woman could not directly avow, her interest in and attraction to a man. A special "language of the fan" developed, in which various poses signaled messages of courtship.

This picture has been dated to around 1880, but given its stylistic and thematic similarities to mid-decade pictures such as *In the Conservatory* (c. 1875; private collection) and *The Bunch of Lilacs* (c. 1875; private collection), it is more likely somewhat earlier.

YALE ONLY

41 *By the Window*, 1875
   Drypoint and etching, 7⁷⁄₁₆ x 4⁵⁄₁₆ in. (W. 9)
   Signed and dated in the plate, upper right; signed in pencil,
      lower margin, left; red monogram stamp, upper right
   Private collection

Holding a closed fan and wearing an elaborate ruffled scarf,
with the ribbons of her hat streaming down her back, the
lady smiles as if in response to a remark by someone outside
the picture space, demonstrating Tissot's interest in captur-
ing the typical gestures and expressions of modern life. Like
his friend Degas, who believed that modernity imprinted
itself on individuals, affecting their movements, their
stances, and even their physiognomies, Tissot wished to
record characteristic attitudes of the people around him;
unlike Degas, he preferred the study of middle- and upper-
class individuals to that of laundresses and dancers. At this
point in his experiments with etching, Tissot was attempting
to use the fewest lines possible, creating a sketchy effect;
in the lady's hat and ruff, he uses drypoint to achieve rich
shadow.

fig. 20. James Tissot, *Decorated fan*, 1872, private collection

no. 41

42 *Ramsgate*, 1876

Drypoint, 9⅝ x 13¾ in. (W. 22)
Signed and dated in the plate, lower right;
   red monogram stamp, lower right
Private collection

In this scene of two women and a man in a hotel overlooking the port of Ramsgate, Tissot reworked a theme he had established in a painting he showed at the International Exhibition of 1872, *Before the Departure* (*The Thames*) (fig. 21). Rather than the smoky, polluted Thames, however, the backdrop here is the man-made harbor of Ramsgate. In both compositions the line of a balcony establishes the unusual diagonal composition of which Tissot was fond, and the man gazes in concern or admiration at a woman who appears to ignore him. In the far edge of each a second woman stands admiring the view, although in *Ramsgate* her attention is distracted by the couple. Whereas the quaint dockside setting and colorful naval character give *Before the Departure* a comic twist, attempting to understand the relationships between the individuals in *Ramsgate* leaves one struggling with misleading clues and an uncertainty as to their mood, which could be one of carefree enjoyment, unrequited love, or some other form of tension.

In this print Tissot may have been subtly acknowledging the English artist William Powell Frith, whose well-known painting of *Ramsgate Sands* (Royal Collection) had astonished visitors to the Royal Academy exhibition of 1854. In the distance on the left appears the famed Ramsgate lighthouse. (Tissot forgot to allow for the reversal that takes place in the etching process; it was actually to the right.) As well as being an important port, Ramsgate was a fashionable resort town, particularly favored by Londoners as a retreat from the pressures of metropolitan life. The medical profession recommended it for ailing patients and convalescents, so perhaps the man and woman are gazing at the seated woman out of concern for her health. Tissot depicted another of England's seaside health resorts in *A Fête Day at Brighton* (c. 1875–78; private collection), and perhaps spent some time in them himself seeking cures for his consumptive model and mistress, Kathleen Newton.

fig. 21. Wood-engraving after Tissot's *Before the Departure* (*The Thames*), from the *Graphic*, February 8, 1873

no. 42

In the Garden

One of the most common settings for Tissot's works was the garden. As evidence of God's miraculous variety and bounty, gardens were spiritually charged locations; the subtexts for the Victorian garden were the Garden of Eden, the Garden of Gethsemane, and the *hortus conclusus*, symbolizing the Virgin Mary. As restful, secular temples in which one could worship both God and his beautiful natural creations, gardens provided a reprieve from the pressures of modern life. One Victorian garden writer declared that there was "more than ever need that our gardens should give back to us some of the pleasures which civilisation and all the ongoing 'way of the world' are stealing from us."[1] Many middle-class home-owners were taking up gardening as a therapeutic activity, designing their own small patches of land as carefully as the landed aristocracy had arranged their large estates. Gardening manuals and journals proliferated, offering advice on an enormous range of topics from the practical (such as the best types of flowers for urban environments) to matters of taste (appropriate color combinations for flowerbeds).

Frequently Tissot painted his own garden, which he designed with a care and attentiveness to detail that made it a work of art in its own right (fig. 22). The distinctive cast-iron colonnade was a reproduction of a marble original in the Parc Monceau, Paris, and it appears in many of his pictures, including *Quarrelling* (no. 43), *Holyday* (no. 45), and *Croquet* (no. 47). The small looking-glass pond that it surrounded was a common feature of suburban gardens, a miniature

fig. 22. Treillage colonnade in Tissot's garden, *Country Life*, November 23, 1912

version of the lakes and ponds of eighteenth-century landscape design.

At first Tissot used the garden as a site of adult social events such as games, picnics, flirtations, and other leisure activities. After the advent of Kathleen Newton around 1876, however, he increasingly concentrated on apparently simple images of women and children, and the later garden pictures are notable for their almost total exclusion of men (see nos. 56, 58–61). Unlike Tissot's urban or Thames-side scenes, these works are flooded with sunshine, a difference that points to the positive meanings the garden held for the artist and his audiences.

no. 43

43 *Quarrelling*, c. 1874–76
   Oil on canvas, 28½ x 19 in.
   The Old House Foundation Ltd.

Looking in different directions, a man and woman stand at
the edge of Tissot's pond on either side of a cast-iron column, while the drooping branches of a weeping willow cascade over the colonnade. As the title makes clear, all is not
well in their relationship, and Tissot has the column stand
in for whatever obstacle has appeared in the course of their
romance. In the background of *Holyday* (no. 45) another
couple idles by this colonnade, although their postures suggest flirtation rather than argument. The woman appears to
be the same model as the one in *Autumn on the Thames*
(*Nuneham Courtney*) (no. 19) and wears an identical
costume.

   The picture bears comparison with Tissot's earlier and
more straightforward *Les Adieux* (no. 4). In both cases the
couples are separated by iron obstacles that are metaphors
for what has come between them in their love. *Les Adieux* is
clearly legible, the tender concern of the young man as
evident as the woman's emotion. In *Quarrelling*, on the other
hand, the man's face is oddly obscured, removing him from
the narrative, and what we can see of the woman's is inscru-
table. In a very modern way Tissot deliberately creates an
ambiguous vignette in which cause and blame are unclear.
After some initial confusion Victorian viewers may have
come to some conclusions all the same; although the weeping
willow was a common symbol of unrequited love, the fact
that the iron column is not actually solid—that nothing truly
substantial separates the pair—suggests that their quarrel
may be resolvable.
   YALE ONLY

44 *The Letter*, c. 1876–78

Oil on canvas, 28¼ x 42¼ in.
Signed and indistinctly dated on base of urn at right
National Gallery of Canada, Ottawa

Striding through a litter of dead horse-chestnut leaves, a stylish young woman, wearing the skirt also seen in *Autumn on the Thames (Nuneham Courtney)* (no. 19) and *Quarrelling* (no. 43), stormily tears up the letter of the title. White fragments flutter to the ground in her wake to mingle with the other "leaves." Rather than following the carefully laid-out paths of the ornamental gardens around her, she moves across the grass, as if to illustrate her disordered state of mind. Behind her a servant places a tray on a table, around which cluster four chairs—perhaps awaiting a guest who has canceled a visit and incurred her wrath.

Pictures in which letters figured prominently were popular with Victorian audiences, who were accustomed to a range of ways narrative could be created in pictorial form. Letters were ideal for this purpose, as they allowed viewers to guess at a story outside of the depicted moment. John Everett Millais's three-part *Yes or No?* series, for instance, depicts women considering marriage proposals. In the Millais series the contents of the letters are quite clear, however, whereas Tissot leaves us in doubt as to what we are witnessing. The apparently headless cupid on the large carved urn behind the woman suggests that her turmoil is related to romance. But is she destroying a rejection of her affections (the canceled visit), a lover's plea, or perhaps evidence of an extramarital affair?

The garden, its splendor fading into fall, is beautifully realized in such details as the curls of dried leaves lining the walks, which contrast sharply with the still-green grass, and the crimson-stained ivy climbing the brick arcade. To savvy Londoners this was not just any garden but the site of a well-known scandal of the period, to which *The Letter* may make subtle reference. The distinctive ivy-covered arches were the remains of seventeenth-century stables in the Dutch Garden at Holland House, the London estate of the Earl of Holland (destroyed in the Second World War).[2]

fig. 23. Dutch Garden, Holland House, from Marie Liechtenstein, *Holland House*, 1874. By permission of The British Library

In 1872 Marie Fox, the French adopted daughter of Lord and Lady Holland, married Prince Louis Aloys Liechtenstein. On looking into his new wife's origins, the prince could not substantiate her parents' vague claims that she was of noble birth; in fact she appeared to have been the out-of-wedlock child of a commoner. As the court of Liechtenstein had strict rules about receiving only aristocrats, the prince was furious; Marie began an acrimonious correspondence with Lady Holland demanding explanations, which, in 1873, caused a lifelong rift between them. Perhaps in *The Letter* Tissot was commenting on the cessation of communication between the new princess and her adoptive parents.

In 1874, at the very moment Lord Holland was attempting to determine the true identity of her natural father, Marie published a two-volume history of the house in which she had grown up, with illustrations of her favorite sites, such as the gardens (fig. 23).[3] In this way she established her claim at least to an English, if not a French, aristocratic background.

no. 44

45 *Holyday*, c. 1877
   Oil on canvas, 30 x 39 in.
   Signed, lower right
   Exhibited: Grosvenor Gallery, 1877
   Tate Gallery, London

Holyday portrays a variety of interactions between men and women. Young couples dominate the picture: one in the background, separated by a column; one under the tree at the left (the woman almost hidden by the man); and a pair in the central foreground. In this last group a man leans against the back of a woman in an attitude of familiarity, suggesting he is connected to her in some way. In the reflection in the teakettle is yet another couple, standing in front of a house on a lawn framed by green trees.

   As the title makes clear, the couples are enjoying a holiday, a time unlike daily, ordinary life, in a vignette defined in relation to what it is not, a scene of labor. We understand that the gentlemen are engaged in a new practice, the scheduling and spending of "time off." Some Victorian social commentators believed that this new category of leisure time led to a disinclination for work and a decline of moral values.[4] Fearful of the deleterious effects of too much unstructured time, some writers advocated taking up the discipline of the playing field in one's free moments. In Tissot's picture the three young men sport that hallmark of modern English upper- and upper-middle-class masculinity, the cricketing cap. The two yellow, black, and red caps are from the prestigious club *I Zingari*, "the gypsies" or "wanderers"; this was of aristocratic origin, having started at Eton around 1845, and was made up of twenty-five gentlemen—as opposed to professional—members.[5] The advocates of sport argued that school and club games would improve the British constitution, instilling discipline, a sense of community, and a willingness to obey. Promoting selflessness, manly combativeness, and sociability, cricket was a modern way of training men for Imperial rule.[6]

   The specimens of English imperial manhood in Tissot's painting are not nobly protecting civilization, however. Rather they lounge lazily in a garden, posing affectedly and dallying with women. The garden space intensifies the interactions between the couples; as secluded, enclosed places, gardens had long been associated with love and courtship.[7] In the garden young men were supposed to find young women with whom to begin families, but *Holyday* invokes this happy narrative only to complicate it.

   By the way he weights the detail of the woman pouring milk into the man's cup, Tissot may be humorously implying that the men are actually in moral danger from their female companions. The curve of the tree branch directly above echoes the interaction between the couple, and the white teacup, slightly askew in its saucer, catches our attention by its central location and brilliance. The woman's gesture, charged by its formal prominence, is captured at the instant before the milk makes contact with the china. Drawn to her hand, we notice that she wears a ring on the third finger and a cameo bearing the likeness of a soldier, presumably her husband. This "clue" points to a missing male who provides the rest of the story, and whom Tissot implicitly contrasts with the effeminate males idling in the garden. While the old lady chaperone dozes, this apparently married woman seems to be initiating a dangerous flirtation.

   The painting is a secular parody of the Fall of Man, in which a modern-day Eve, her long serpentine tresses escaping confinement, proffers temptation in the form of milk for Adam's tea. A snake figure—the dragon on the teapot—appears to threaten the man, completing the symbolic analogy. Tissot was later to produce overtly religious scenes set in his own era, *The Prodigal Son in Modern Life* (see nos. 72–75), and once stated, "the more I acquire…the more I desire and the more hopefully I strive, to produce compositions that reveal the hidden meanings of our everyday life."[8] *Holyday* appears to have been an experiment in representing modern life in a meaningful, substantive way, drawing on popular culture but anchored to traditional artistic themes.

no. 45

46 *The Widower*, 1877

Oil on canvas, 46½ x 30¼ in.
Exhibited: Grosvenor Gallery, 1877
Art Gallery of New South Wales, Australia
Gift of Sir Colin and Lady Anderson, 1939

Like *Spring* (no. 51), *The Widower* is a vertical composition of figures standing behind foreground foliage. In this case tall irises, reeds, and a strange flowering rhubarb plant block our access to the middle-aged bearded man of the title, who holds up his little girl so that she may pluck what appears to be a still unripe nut from a tree. Such use of greenery to frame a figure was common in Japanese prints, which Tissot collected and occasionally emulated.[9] The girl was probably modeled by Violet Newton, Kathleen's daughter, who would have been about six at the time, but the scenario of the picture is fictional rather than actual. Both figures wear mourning attire, indicating that the wife and mother has been dead for less than a year, although the girl has a white pinafore and a checked sash over her somber dress. The solemn, careworn expression on the man's face as he holds the remaining member of his family struck a chord for Victorian audiences, who were fond of sentimental representations of death and mourning. "*The Widower* has already become popular for its pathetic sentiment," noted one reviewer.[10] Even the hard-to-please playwright and aesthete Oscar Wilde praised the work, though for its pictorial rather than emotional qualities,

saying it was "full of depth and suggestiveness; the grasses and wild luxuriant growth to the foreground are a revel of natural life."[11]

The striking opposition of the verdant vegetation and the stark blacks and whites of the mourning attire underlines the sad contrast between the sorrowing people and the vitality of the burgeoning season; as one critic recognized, "the rich summer vegetation is rife with thoughts of the summers that once brought blossoms of life and joy to him."[12] Although Tissot's gardens usually celebrated love or the pleasures of childhood, he also occasionally used them as sites in which to explore the melancholy themes of illness and death. As places where the natural life cycle played itself out despite careful human management, perhaps gardens seemed appropriate settings in which to contemplate mortality. In *The Widower* the child, fruit of the severed union, grabs at the fruit of the tree, reminding the viewer that humans also bear and die. According to Christian belief, however, the wife will be reborn like the earth, so the lush summer green is not only pathetic but also suggests the immortality of the soul.

no. 46

47 *Croquet*, c. 1878

Oil on canvas, 35⅜ x 20 in.
Exhibited: Grosvenor Gallery, 1878
Art Gallery of Hamilton, Ontario
Gift of Dr. and Mrs. Basil Bowman
in memory of their daughter Suzanne, 1965

Three adolescent girls occupy a sunlit garden space, contained by the distinctive iron colonnade of Tissot's own garden and a road in the distance, which creates a sense of secure enclosure. One demurely smiling girl kneels and gazes at the grass, as if lost in private thoughts, while another looks out at us as she lolls childlike on the ground. The oldest of the three stands in the foreground holding a croquet mallet, although the other two have taken up neither playing equipment nor positions. This girl poses provocatively, hips thrust forward and to one side, with her mallet stretched behind her back and delicately balanced across two fingers of her right hand. Extending up the right side and arching over the vertical canvas is a tree that forms a pictorial gateway into the sunlit world. The girl gazing at us appears to invite us from our shadowy space to join the game or, perhaps, given the ball in the foreground, to make our next move. Since the small dog is undisturbed, our presence is presumably familiar and unthreatening.

Introduced from France around 1860, croquet was a popular amusement of the leisured classes at this time, favored for the opportunities it allowed for unchaperoned contact and flirtation between young men and women. As a manual for the game commented, "one of the greatest charms of the game of croquet is the sight it offers of a neatly-turned pair of ankles."[13] The girl in *Croquet* does reveal this part of her body; she is too young to have lengthened her skirts and put up her hair, but clearly she is on the verge of womanhood. Given the connotations of croquet, perhaps this young miss is flirting with the viewer. She stands at the edge of a garden in which the other children, uninvolved in the game with its adult resonances, sit more passively; indeed, rather than inviting us in with her, she is poised to step out of her paradise into the adult world of sexuality.

Tissot's familiarity with Impressionist technique and understanding of color is evident in his brilliant depiction of sunshine on verdant lawn. The individual brushstrokes, which become more pronounced as the picture space recedes —in the blue-green patches to the left of the girl in the shadow, for example—draw attention to the artist's touch and flatten out the canvas, preventing a wholly convincing effect of three-dimensionality.

Tissot was fond enough of this composition to paint a watercolor replica (Rhode Island School of Design) and to feature it on a vase when he designed some cloisonné work (c. 1882; Musée des Arts Décoratifs, Paris).

no. 47

48 *A Children's Garden Party*, 1880
    Drypoint, 10¹⁄₁₆ x 6⅜ in.
    Second state (W. 49, ɪɪ/ɪɪ)
    Signed in the plate, lower right; signed in pencil,
       lower margin, left; red monogram stamp, lower right
    Private collection

This drypoint relates closely to *In the Sunlight* (no. 58), containing the same Japanese sunshade, both collapsed and open, fur rug, and women in bonnets and black dresses. By using drypoint alone rather than combining it with etching as he usually did, Tissot makes his design more casual and lively. He experiments with depicting motion and instantaneous poses, such as the action of the seated lady on the left who turns to speak with her child or the humorous mugging of the little boy staring out at us in the foreground. His loose handling of the foliage in the background, which consists of patches of diagonal lines and crosshatching, contributes to this sense of spontaneity.

The youngest child with the woman on the left is Reginald Hervey, Kathleen Newton's nephew, and the woman is perhaps her sister Mary Hervey, with her daughter Belle also by her side. The other children are Mary's daughter Lilian under the umbrella and Cecil Newton, who appears at the back of the group with his mother and again in the front.

Tissot painted an oil, *The Children's Garden Party* (private collection), that shows the same characters in a different composition. Interestingly, some of the same props had also appeared in his earlier portrayal of a picnic, *Holyday* (no. 45). The comparison with *Holyday* illustrates what very different activities can occur on a lawn; perhaps Tissot was drawing a humorous contrast between adult flirtation and the innocent childish enjoyment of a *déjeuner sur l'herbe*.

no. 48

49 *Le Petit Nemrod (The Little Nimrod)*, 1886
Mezzotint, 16⅝ x 22¹⁄₁₆ in.
First state, without title below (W. 83, I/II)
Signed in the plate, lower right; signed in pencil, lower margin, left
Private collection

On a path in a formal garden lined with horse-chestnut trees, a young boy on a hobby horse pretends to slaughter wild animals in the form of girls draped with tiger and lion skins. At first the work appears to be merely a vignette of happy childhood romping. Yet play itself was serious. Victorian educators and childhood experts believed that a child passively absorbed the experiences to which she or he was exposed.[14] Seemingly carefree playtime activities were thought to shape the growing consciousness and contribute to future self-discipline and development.

Chillingly, the activities that the children mimic are killing and dying. The boy, posed by Kathleen Newton's son Cecil, is acting out the role of the biblical Nimrod, a warrior and hunter, replacing his sword after having "killed" all three "animals" that were presumably menacing him.[15] Slaughtering the animals represented by the girls, the boy is the main active figure in the image, creating a marked dichotomy between the roles of the male and female children. Such a distinction was common in Victorian art. Play, and representations of play, were influential reinforcers of gender roles. Playing at killing animals teaches the boy about the appropriateness of blood sport in the life of an English gentleman; implicitly it also compares the hierarchy of male over female to that of man over animal.

Here Cecil takes a step on the road to an independent masculine identity. The boy symbolically slays his childish, feminized self in the person of the girls, separating himself from the female realm of the garden in the same way that he has abandoned skirts for trousers. Tissot appears to have been very interested in the maturation process of the model in these pictures; in an etching entitled *His First Breeches* (fig. 24), he shows Cecil standing staunchly at the foot of a staircase, as if ready to ascend the steps of life. While there is no substantive proof, Tissot might actually have been Cecil's father. If this is indeed the case, the painter is representing his own son growing into an adult Victorian male, in a covert acknowledgment and celebration of his paternity. Such a personal connection may explain why *Le Banc de jardin* (no. 61) and *Le Petit Nemrod* seem to have had particular meaning for the artist; they are two of only four mezzotints he created, and he kept the painted version of *Le Banc de jardin* in his possession until his death.

Just as *Le Petit Nemrod* marked Cecil's step away from his mother, perhaps it was also Tissot's declaration of independence from the academic tradition of art. In its theme of man and animal in combat and its conventional pyramidal composition, it echoes Salon works such as Horace Vernet's *Lion Hunt* of 1835 (fig. 25). But Tissot turns the hunters and lions into frolicking children, implying that the difficult work of history painting was for him mere child's play. He asserts the relevance and artistic seriousness of modern-life subjects, at the same time deflating the pretensions of *la grande peinture*.

fig. 24. James Tissot, *His First Breeches*, 1880 Drypoint, 7 x 3 in. (W. 51), Art Gallery of Ontario, Toronto, Gift of Allan and Sondra Gotlieb, 1994

no. 49

fig. 25. Horace Vernet, *Lion Hunt*, 1835
Oil on canvas, 22½ x 32⅛ in.
The Wallace Collection, London

The Seasons

In 1878 Tissot began a series of works in which women embodied the seasons, a traditional theme in Western art. Rather than draping them in the conventional classical robes, however, Tissot made his figures insistently modern by dressing them in the latest fashions. Only the titles cued the viewer that the pictures were allegories. To *July* (no. 52) and the oil version of *Spring* (see no. 51), moreover, the artist added the subtitle "specimen of a portrait," so that they became not only allegories—representations of ideas—but also portraits, representations of individuals. Taking on the oxymoronic status of "allegorical portraiture," the works vacillated between two poles, the general and the particular; with them, Tissot attempted to create a new category, a specifically modern allegory. Perhaps he was inspired by the allegorical and mystical work of the Pre-Raphaelite painter Edward Burne-Jones, which he saw on a studio visit in 1875. He later confessed to Burne-Jones's widow: "I sensed the heights where he soared and the materiality where I struggled more and more in those days."[1]

As in his earlier society pictures, Tissot bolstered his project by drawing on popular culture. These works appear to have been a series, meant to be understood in relationship to one another as well as individually. Taken together, they resemble a fashion magazine, each plate illustrating the correct, up-to-date costume for each season. Since their first appearance Tissot's paintings have been identified with fashion to such an extent that art and dress historians have relied on them to reconstruct actual clothing. One contemporary writer even believed that the painter set fashion trends himself, remarking, "at the present time in England Mr. James Tissot and Mr. George Du Maurier exercise considerable control over the fashions"; in turn, fashion magazines would occasionally promote Tissot's work.[2] Reviewers frequently likened his paintings to fashion plates (see fig. 26), a mass art form which had exploded as technology improved and modes changed more and more rapidly. As one critic remarked, "his devotion to modern millinery in its most extravagant forms lends an ephemeral fashion-book air to

fig. 26. Plate from *The Ladies' Treasury*, February 1877

his performances."[3] Such observations arose from visual cues such as his obsessive attention to the details of costume, the shallow spaces of his compositions, and the remote air of his models.

Tissot concentrated on fashion in part because its details and varied fabrics gave him a chance to display his technical virtuosity, in part because he subscribed to Charles Baudelaire's and the Impressionists' belief that the representation of modernity required a careful observation of contemporary costume.[4] In creating paintings that addressed popular visual culture—fashion plates, illustrated newspapers, and photographs—he was participating in a self-consciously avant-garde practice.[5] Unlike popular color lithographs and engravings, oil painting was traditionally reserved for more permanent subject matter; involving it in the realm of the mass, the fleeting, the commercial, and the cheap was a transgressive act.

50 *October*, 1878

Etching and drypoint, 21¹¹⁄₁₆ x 10⅞ in. (W. 33)

Signed and dated in the plate, upper right; signed in pencil,
   lower margin, right; red monogram stamp, lower margin, right

Private collection

Etched after a painting of the same title modeled by Kathleen
Newton(1877; Museum of Fine Arts, Montreal), this work
depicts a woman walking in an autumnal park, swiveling
outward to observe the reaction elicited by the display of her
ankles beneath her hitched-up petticoats. The feet of middle-
class Victorian women, rarely glimpsed in public, were a
focus of considerable erotic attention; numerous jokes,
caricatures and fictional accounts drew attention to the fact.
The popular novelist G. J. Whyte-Melville, of whom Tissot
made a caricature (fig. 2), described one of his gentlemen
characters pausing before a pair of ladies' boots left in a
hallway for cleaning: "it was obvious they belonged to a very
pretty foot, slim and supple, hollow and arched…For a man
who admired pretty feet it was impossible to pass those boots
without further examination" —which, in this case, was to
include kissing them.[6]

The shoes worn by the young woman in *October* are
daringly fashionable high heels, which forced their wearer
into the walking posture known as "the Grecian Bend," tilted
forward with the derrière emphasized by a bustle. With her
chic doubled-up braid, probably made of fake hair, hint of
petticoat, and apparently cosmetic-lined eyes (more obvious
in the painted version), she resembles caricatures of the
young woman known as the "girl of the period," a phrase
coined after an influential series of articles in the *Saturday
Review*. In a diatribe against modern fashions, the author
lamented the fact that respectable girls were aping the
appearance of prostitutes and claimed that men, lured by
false advertising, were choosing inappropriate mates: "If each
separate point of female attire and decoration is a sham, so
the whole is often a deception and a fraud…Thus it comes to
be a grave matter of doubt, when a man marries, how much
is real of the woman who became his wife."[7]

Here Tissot demonstrates his ability to create an etching
in which black dominates yet does not obscure the nuances

no. 50

of modeling. Surrounding the woman in a delicate all-over
pattern is his trademark horse-chestnut foliage, and she
walks on a ground strewn with leaves fallen from above.
To the left in the distance a herd of deer stand at attention,
the large antlers of a stag pinpointing the season.

51 *Spring*, 1878
    Etching and drypoint, 14¹⁵⁄₁₆ x 5⅜ in. (W. 34)
    Signed in the plate, upper right;
        red monogram stamp, upper right
    Private collection

The model wears the same ruffled white dress shown in *July*
(no. 52), with the season suggested only by the blooming
rhododendron in the background and the apple blossoms
cascading elegantly down the upper part of the picture plane.
Hand on hip, she holds her fan behind her shoulder in
another of Tissot's studies of the deployment of this feminine
accessory. Also as in *July* Tissot experiments with backlight-
ing. In a difficult maneuver for an etcher, he delicately
delineates the edges of the dress and the woman's face in
white while casting the center of her body in shadow.

    In its flatness and slightly iconic appearance, *Spring* re-
sembles a fashion plate more than any other of Tissot's
seasonal images. With his interest in making pictures that
did not clearly tell a story, he found the fashion plate admi-
rably suited to his needs as a format to imitate; it had no
reason to exist other than to display a product to its best
advantage, and depicted women for the sake of their appearance alone, outside of any narrative. Tissot was also influenced by the work of artists of the Aesthetic Movement, such
as Dante Gabriel Rossetti, whose images of women gaze out
at the viewer and are intended to be contemplated for their
beauty rather than for any moral or story.

no. 51

52 *July: Specimen of a Portrait*, c. 1878
   Oil on canvas, 34½ x 23¼ in.
   Signed, upper left
   Exhibited: possibly Grosvenor Gallery, 1878
   Cleveland Museum of Art. Bequest of Noah L. Butkin

In the delicate, airy *July* the model lounges on a sofa in a fashionable seaside resort; in the background is a sketchy beach scene reminiscent of those by Claude Monet. Subtly backlit, her cheeks catching the outdoor glare that filters through the red-and-white-striped awning, the woman represents the sun-filled month with her excessive yellow ribbons and golden pillows. The floral pattern on the sofa similarly evokes the luxuriant gardens of high summer.

The light muslin dress, an appropriate outfit for the season, appears in several other pictures by Tissot, including *The Gallery of H.M.S. Calcutta* (no. 28), suggesting that it was a studio prop. The artist's collection of dresses reflected his seriousness about that most frivolous of social elements, fashion. Not only did he wish to record actual, individual gowns, he also chose them carefully, only a few suiting his aesthetic sense.

Although the model for this painting appears to have been Kathleen Newton, the vibrant red hair differs from that in other representations of her. X-ray analysis reveals yellow paint underneath the red and a substantial repainting of this area; it has even been suggested that it was worked by a later hand to suit the taste or interior decor of a collector.[8]

no. 52

53 *A Winter's Walk*, 1880
     Etching and drypoint, 22⅛ x 10½ in.
     Second state, with text printed in red (W. 48, II/III)
     Signed and dated in the plate, lower right;
        red monogram stamp, lower right
     Private collection

When exhibited in Manchester in 1878, the painted version
of *A Winter's Walk* (private collection) was described as "a
fairy form enveloped in furs, out of which we have a peep
of a sweet and enticing face."[9] For the final work in Tissot's
series of seasons, Kathleen Newton poses once again, wearing
a huge fur collar and muff. Under the print the artist includes
a line from Keats's poem "Fancy": "She will bring in spite of
frost / Beauties that the earth hath lost," suggesting the idea
of her youthful vitality challenging the frozen landscape. Illustrating the stark contrasts of wintertime, her velvety black
stole stands out against the flat white of the snow. Behind
the woman an evergreen, symbolizing the eternal aspect
of nature, which will rejuvenate in the spring, spreads its
branches in a virtuoso display of Tissot's talents as an etcher.

During his lifetime Tissot's etchings were more consis-
tently admired than his paintings, and he was included in
numerous compilations and reference works on this technique. As a painter who etched his own work, he was unusual. Far from being rote copies of his pictures by other hands,
his etchings are original works of art in their own right.

Although many of the tributes to Tissot imply that he did
his own printing, he actually sent his plates to the renowned
English printer Frederick Goulding. He began to work with
Goulding as soon as he became serious about etching,
appearing in the printer's logbooks in 1875, and continued to
do so throughout his career as a printmaker.[10] In a letter to a
friend in 1881, he complained that Goulding could only see
him one day a week, if that, attesting to the demand for the
man's skills.[11] After Tissot returned to Paris in the 1880s,
Goulding visited and worked with him there, clearly having
come to value their relationship.[12]

She will bring in spite of frost
Beauties that the earth hath lost. Keats.

no. 53

no. 54

Declarations of Love

From 1877 onward Tissot painted and etched many scenes featuring his new, soon almost ubiquitous model, Kathleen Irene Kelly Newton. She was a divorced Irishwoman who lived nearby in St. John's Wood and moved into Tissot's house some time around 1876. In March of that year she had a son, Cecil George Newton, who may have been Tissot's child. Certainly Tissot and Newton seem to have been lovers, although they never married. The reason usually given for this is that they were both devout Catholics, and her status as a divorcée would have prevented it, but possibly Tissot did not want to lower himself by marrying a woman with an unsavory past. In 1870, engaged to a man she barely knew, Kathleen Kelly (as she then was) had an affair with a soldier on the journey to join her fiancé in India. Probably pregnant with the soldier's child, she went through with the marriage, but her husband initiated divorce proceedings as soon as her pregnancy became visible in May 1871. She returned to England to have the child, a daughter, whom she registered as Muriel Mary Violet Newton. When the artist met her, she was living with her married sister, Mary Hervey. Tissot's illicit relationship seems to have affected his welcome in polite English society, and until Newton's death from tuberculosis in 1882 he withdrew to his own smaller, more tolerant Bohemian circles.

Tissot depicted Newton at the same sites he had found attractive before—particularly along the Thames, in the garden, and in the streets of London. A new category of setting appeared as well, that of the domestic space inhabited by women and children. It is hard to resist reading the paintings for which Newton posed in a biographical way, seeing them as records of the couple's passion and happiness, and searching for signs of her wasting illness. But we should be wary of the subjectivity of this sort of analysis. Writers on Tissot have said of the very same work: "it clearly shows that she did not have long to live" and "there is no indication of the hovering shadow of illness that was to claim her life the following year."[1]

Certainly some of the images of Newton appear more personal than others, but we must remember that Tissot did not create them solely as private records of his family life. He was intent on earning an income with these productions, many of which went to exhibitions or art dealers. *Quiet* (no. 60), for example, appeared at the Royal Academy in 1881, the year before Newton died. If Tissot made pictures of her as intimate, poignant mementos, how could he have borne to expose them to such public scrutiny?

54 *Waiting for the Ferry*, c. 1878
Oil on panel, 9¼ x 14¼ in.
Signed, lower left
Private collection

The scene in *Waiting for the Ferry* is set at Gravesend, on the Thames estuary east of London, in front of the Old Falcon Hotel. Gravesend, or "Tombs-Beginning" as it was jocularly termed, was a site of holiday leisure for tired Londoners. Once the railway was built in the 1850s, it was only an hour away from the center of the city and cheaply accessible; tourists could take a train to Tilbury station and catch the ferry steamer to the other side of the river. There they could watch shipping, enjoy the famous taverns, or stroll the busy pier.

The models for the figures were Kathleen Newton and her brother Frederick, her son Cecil, and her niece Lilian. In a photograph he appears to have used in constructing the painting (fig. 27), Tissot himself occupies the place later taken by Frederick. The photograph shows Tissot as older, darker, rounder of face, and blunter of nose than the man he painted. On the other hand, the strange obscuring of the man's features suggests that, on some level, Tissot was actually portraying himself in his intimate relationship with Newton, in a form of disguised self-portraiture.

The group in the painting seems to be a family waiting for the ferry on their way home, the mother somewhat disengaged or bored, the father protectively clinging to his boy. The boy looks sulky, and the girl is separated from the rest of the group, her tourist's vision obstructed by the railing. Perhaps, Tissot implies, the new form of river tourism did not live up to the promise of the guidebooks.

For another version of *Waiting for the Ferry*, without the children and with Newton wearing a veil, see fig. 5.

YALE AND QUEBEC ONLY

fig. 27. Photograph of the artist with Kathleen Newton, her son Cecil, and her niece Lilian Hervey

55 *Richmond Bridge (Declaration of Love)*, c. 1878

Oil on panel, 11½ x 7¾ in.
Signed, lower right
Collection Felix Abada, New York

Closely related to *Waiting for the Ferry* (no. 54), *Richmond Bridge* was also painted around 1878 and features figures modeled by Kathleen Newton and her brother Frederick. Richmond, to the west of London, was a popular destination for short day trips from the city. Described as a place of "repose and recreation within an hour's railway ride of dusty, noisy streets and wearisome bustle of social vanity or commercial greed," it was famous for its landscape scenery.[2] Built by James Paine in 1779, its well-known bridge was admired for its graceful, classical proportions.

The narrative of Tissot's picture seems to revolve around the stability of marriage and the family. Apparently compelled to express his feelings, the man is writing with his stick in the sand: "I love you." The woman smiles as she sees the message. In this way the picture literally spells out its theme, to all appearances that of married love.

Again like *Waiting for the Ferry*, the composition seems to have been based on photographs in which Frederick's part is played by Tissot himself; even if the features are Frederick's in the painting, it seems highly likely that Tissot was thinking of himself. His stand-in is, after all, using his stick to engrave the canvas with a message of love. The stick stands in for the artist's brush: the artist confesses his feelings only to disguise them by attributing them to another man.

During this period of their life together Newton was slipping away from Tissot, dying of tuberculosis, and perhaps he felt an urgent need to capture her, and his desire for her, in paint. Certainly *Waiting for the Ferry* and *Richmond Bridge* seem more personal than most of his works. Their small scale endows them with a less public, more intimate address as though they were intended for an audience familiar with the relationships between the people depicted and the artist.

no. 55

no. 56

56 *The Hammock*, 1880
Etching and drypoint, 10⅞ x 7¼ in. (W. 46)
Signed and dated in the plate, lower left
Private collection

This etching belongs to a group of works, including three paintings shown at the Grosvenor Gallery exhibition of 1879, that show Kathleen Newton wearing a fashionable black dress and swinging in a hammock in Tissot's garden in St. John's Wood. Although no reviewers of the Grosvenor exhibition identified Newton, they appear to have recognized the location as suburban London. As one writer commented, these were "pictures of the 'detached villa' kind."[3] (The phrase refers to the distinctive architectural type of the newly emergent suburbs, the freestanding house.) Despite their apparently innocuous subjects the pictures in question were savaged by the critics. One fumed, "this year [Tissot] tries our patience somewhat hardly, for these ladies in hammocks, showing a very unnecessary amount of petticoat and stocking, and remarkable for little save luxurious indolence and insolence, are hardly fit subjects for such elaborate painting."[4] To determine why the pictures evoked such anxiety, we need to re-examine the meaning of the phrase "pictures of the 'detached villa' kind."

The humorous magazine *Punch* identified Tissot's setting as St. John's Wood and, perhaps insinuating intimate knowledge of Tissot's personal life—he was, after all, living with Newton outside of matrimony—referred to this suburb in a way that reminded the informed reader that, in addition to being a domain of domesticity, it was also famous for fashionable kept women. As one commentator darkly proclaimed, the female inhabitants of the area were composed of "divorced wives, not married to anyone in particular, mysterious widows whose husbands have never been seen, married women whose better halves were engaged in the City."[5]

Had Tissot overtly represented a prostitute and her clients, his painting would not have been sanctioned by an Establishment institution such as the Grosvenor. Indeed, he seems to have taken some steps to prevent his model being read in this way: in at least one of his Grosvenor pictures—as in the present etching—Newton is clearly wearing a wedding ring. Apparently neither this sign of respectability nor the presence of innocent children playing in the background were enough to render the situation above reproach.

For many Victorians the new suburbs were not peaceful havens of domesticity but unintelligible and rather threatening products of the modern age. In 1883 an article in the *Architect* referred to them as a "*terra incognita*," comparing them to the American prairie and their inhabitants to pioneers in a "perfect wilderness."[6] The speedy growth of the suburbs meant that it was more difficult to define or comprehend suburb and city alike, given the confusion as to where one began and the other left off. The blurring of the previously clear-cut categories of "city" and "country" also prevented the easy description of this novel landscape. Thus the suburban garden became a defining, deceptively attractive element.

The ambiguity of the woman in Tissot's hammock pictures, whose identity as a respectable bourgeois wife was open to question, was inflected by and in turn contributed to the potential disruptiveness of her suburban garden surroundings. According to the reviewer for the *Illustrated London News*, these images portrayed "the St. John's-Wood life in conservatory or garden (where the London soot seems to be fast penetrating)," implying with this graphic metaphor that the domain of suburbia had been infiltrated by urban vice.[7]

57 *Hide and Seek*, 1880–82
    Oil on panel, 30 x 23¾ in.
    Signed, lower right
    National Gallery of Art, Washington
    Chester Dale Fund

Set in Tissot's luxurious studio, *Hide and Seek* portrays a group of girls occupied in a familiar children's game. The little girl in the white dress with red bows seems to be "It" and has just finished counting, while three other faces in the background peer out at her (and us) in mischievous expectation. In the background Kathleen Newton reads by the window, the tea tray with two cups perched on the armchair hinting at shared social routines. This picture resembles *Le Petit Nemrod* (no. 49) in that both works treat the theme of child's play. Unlike the sunny space of the garden in *Le Petit Nemrod*, however, the world of the little girls and the woman is a gloomy interior, the sense of enclosure exaggerated by the lattices reflected in the glass-covered painting on an easel over the woman's shoulder and the oval mirror on the back wall. The girls are in a sort of pictorial cage, all notional exits, including that of the conservatory on the right, literally barred. Even the parquet floor resembles a grid. To be female is to be contained in the domestic space. Whereas the boy in *Le Petit Nemrod* learns the active role of combat, the girls perform the repetitive, formulaic game of seeking each other out in the home, prefiguring their own future social "calls."

Hide and Seek is also a picture of the artist's own studio, a fact of which we are reminded by the easel in the background. In a sense, therefore, it is a self-portrait, conveying a particular artistic identity. Not surprisingly for one so anxious to establish his credentials as a gentleman, Tissot portrays his studio as a symbol of what he has achieved by his art rather than as a site for creativity itself. Hung from the frame of the easel are exotic masks, which, combined with the furs, rugs, and Japanese and Chinese porcelain, create an image of the owner of this space as a sophisticated, financially secure connoisseur. The conservatory in particular symbolizes Tissot's status as a wealthy modern gentleman in suburban London; with the perfection of glass-and-iron construction techniques, by the 1870s attached greenhouses had become common in the villas of this area.[8]

Tissot's studio is a place of child's play and quiet domesticity rather than furious industry or mystical inspiration; he implies that his art derives from these elements of everyday life rather than from the exalted realms of history or literature.

no. 57

58 *In the Sunlight*, 1881

Etching and drypoint, 7⅞ x 11¾ in. (W. 54)
Signed in the plate, lower left; signed in pencil,
   lower margin, left; red monogram stamp, lower margin, right
Private collection

As usual, Tissot made this etching after one of his own paintings. In this case, however, he modified the design; although the arrangement of the women and children is the same, the background is a simple garden bed rather than the long *allée* shown in the original oil, and the lawn to the lower left is strewn with the children's toys, giving it a less formal appearance.[9] The figure of the woman sitting on the edge of a fur rug in the foreground derives from a photograph of Kathleen Newton. The black cat contentedly basking in the middle of the path may have been a reference to Newton, who was affectionately known as "Kitty."

Newton's daughter Violet modeled for the girl lying on her stomach looking out at the viewer, and her niece Lilian is curled up under a parasol sucking her thumb. To the left another woman, apparently a second portrait of Newton, sits on the wall.[10] As she is sewing, hatless, and less elegantly dressed than the idle woman, perhaps she is meant to represent a servant or governess. Newton's son Cecil posed for the boy leaning against this woman's lap, a ball tucked under his arm.

The title of the work underscores the importance of sunlight to Vicorian citydwellers. The text accompanying Tissot's etching when it was published explained that urban children in particular required this type of nourishment: "The sunshine is doubly prized, where cloud and smoke and fog have their own forbidding way for the best part of the year; especially do children love to bask in its warmth and light."[11] These children engage the viewer with their happy, candid glances, demonstrating carefree enjoyment of the secure, attractive garden space.

Tissot may have intended this work as an homage to James McNeill Whistler, a pioneer of the etching revival, who had portrayed a woman with a parasol in an etching entitled *En plein soleil* (1858). He may also have worked alongside his

fig. 28. Giuseppe de Nittis, "Etude de jeune femme," from the *Gazette des Beaux-Arts*, June 1883

friend the Italian artist Giuseppe de Nittis when painting the original image; de Nittis produced a drawing that strikingly resembles Tissot's depiction of Newton in the etching, showing the same bonnet and costume (fig. 28).

Nineteenth-century painters frequently used the garden as a space in which to explore their family relationships, using their spouses and children as models. Tissot's intense interest in images of mothers and children in gardens (they dominated his output for four years) may have to do with the nostalgic association of gardens with childhood. As an expatriate, he was doubly removed from his own youth, by time and geography. His own mother had died when he was twenty-five, yet he apparently maintained a sentimental connection to her; one contemporary recorded that the first picture he exhibited was a portrait of his mother, which still hung in his studio in 1881.[12] Thinking of his homeland and his mother, perhaps he made paintings of his own garden in compensation, portraying both the land of his adopted country and his new family, including a mother figure.

59 *The Elder Sister*, 1881
   Etching and drypoint, 11⅜ x 6 in. (W. 53)
   Signed and dated in the plate, upper center; signed in pencil,
      lower margin, left; red monogram stamp, lower margin, right
   Private collection

This etching relates to three similar oils of the same subject,
suggesting that the theme especially appealed to the artist. By
entitling it *The Elder Sister*, he reassigns the real-life relationships between the models, in this case Kathleen Newton and
her niece Lilian Hervey. It was a practice of which he was
fond; a painting called *The Orphan*, for instance (1879;
private collection), shows this same pair dressed in black,
although neither had been orphaned in real life. These
images are not portraits but narratives in which Tissot's
models act out roles. Perhaps he was anxious not to reveal
the actual family ties within his circle out of a concern for
their privacy; perhaps he felt that a picture of an aunt with
her niece was less interesting than one of two sisters.
    Despite the fact that the photograph after which Tissot
composed the image depicted the two on an outdoor staircase, here they sit on the carpeted steps of his conservatory,
surrounded on either side by luxuriant foliage. The tiny
narcissi on the right resemble the flowers on the woman's
dress, suggesting her affinity with the hothouse environment.
    Sucking her thumb, Lilian slouches against Newton, who
looks up from reading her a story. Lilian has her thumb in
her mouth in a number of other works, including *In the
Sunlight* (no. 58). This was an unusual pose for children in
high art. Perhaps Tissot chose it for this very reason, seeing
it as a characteristically childish action that had escaped
representation because of its triviality; with his interest in the
details of modern life, he would have reveled in its pettiness.
It was a gesture that captured the relaxed informality and
childish pleasure of the domestic garden space.

no. 59

60 *Quiet*, c. 1881

Oil on canvas, 27 x 36 in.
Signed in monogram, lower right
Exhibited: Royal Academy, 1881
Private collection

A young woman and a little girl sit outside on a fur-covered bench, an attentive black-and-white dog affectionately draping its paw over the girl's waist. Behind them is a sunny garden and the border of Tissot's reflecting pool. The lady has removed her bonnet, which is now poised over the dog's head in a visual pun. Modeling for this work are, again, Kathleen Newton and her niece Lilian; and the bonnet, pillows, and fur rug are the same props that appear in numerous other works of the same time, including *In the Sunlight* (no. 58).

One critic, repulsed by this apparently innocuous painting, claimed that the woman's look "reminds one of 'la Lyre cassée.'"[13] The "broken lyre" might symbolize unstrung sanity or possibly a sullied reputation. Although difficult to explain fully, the hostile reception may have been a reaction to certain perceived improprieties in the picture. Newton's flowing, lace-trimmed blue gown is too low-cut for respectable daytime wear, a fact to which Tissot calls attention with a nosegay of nasturtiums, the orange standing out beautifully against the complementary bright blue. The dark, smudged lines around the woman's eyes suggest that he intended to show his model's use of cosmetics, a controversial practice among members of the middle classes. Though frequently condemned, makeup may have been more prevalent than scholars have assumed, given the number of periodical articles and marketing pamphlets that discuss it frankly. In openly rendering cosmetics in his paintings, Tissot celebrated the appearance of modernity. In this regard he was surely influenced by the art critic and poet Charles Baudelaire, who approved of the use of makeup, asserting that "red and black [rouge and eyeliner] represent life, a supernatural and excessive life: its black frame renders the glance more penetrating and individual, and gives the eye a more decisive appearance of a window open upon the infinite." For him the cosmetic mask "adds to the face of a beautiful woman the mysterious passion of the priestess."[14]

To contemporary viewers of the Royal Academy exhibition of 1881, at which this picture and *Goodbye (On the Mersey)* (no. 37) were Tissot's last appearance, *Quiet* was too mundane and straightforward in its subject to be truly artistic. As one critic demanded, "where is the grace, the character, the excellence of the work with which modern life is to be redeemed if it is to pass into Art?"[15]

no. 60

61 *Le Banc de jardin* (*The Garden Bench*), 1883
   Mezzotint, 16½ x 22⁵⁄₁₆ in.
   Bon à tirer proof (W. 75, I/III)
   Signed in the plate, lower left; signed and
      inscribed "Bon à Tirer," in pencil, lower margin, left
   Private collection

This is the mezzotint version of a painting of the same title. The models for the composition were Kathleen Newton, her daughter Violet, her niece Belle, and her son Cecil, who are arranged on a bench in Tissot's own garden. The boy stands out from his environment, the focus of his mother, who gazes at him adoringly with her back turned to the girls. As in the related work, *Le Petit Nemrod* (no. 49), Cecil is vertical while the girls sprawl horizontally, their floral dresses, like that of the woman, linking them to the exuberant gardens behind them.[16]

Beginning with the Madonna and Child, there was a long tradition of Western imagery depicting women and children in gardens. Further to the religious connotations of this familiar and appealing theme, scientific and social discourses promoted the idea that infants and females were more closely tied to the natural world. The garden was a feminine, nurturing space, related to the helplessness and irresponsibility of childhood and symbolizing the protection of a mother's love. As a boy, Cecil must learn to leave the feminized garden space—literally and symbolically—in order to mature into a man. In *Le Banc de jardin*, although he is differentiated from the girls, he still clings tightly to his mother, requiring adult support to maintain his balance. In *Le Petit Nemrod*, he seems to take a step on the road to independence.

Le Banc de jardin and *Le Petit Nemrod*, both completed after Newton's death and Tissot's departure from England, have a similar haunting quality, created in part by the technique of mezzotint itself. Tissot would have been working from memory, a practice in which he rarely engaged, which may also have contributed to the way in which light, playful moments emerge as solemn and ghostly.

no. 61

62 *L'Apparition médiunimique (The Apparition)*, 1885

Mezzotint, 19⁵⁄₁₆ x 13½ in.
Second state, with title (W. 76, II/II); printed in blue-black ink
Signed and dated in the plate, lower left; red monogram stamp, lower right
Private collection

Tissot created this unusual image after an oil painting inspired by a séance held by the well-known English medium William Eglinton. It depicts the ghost of Kathleen Newton with her spirit guide "Ernest" as she appeared to Tissot and four others on the night of May 20, 1885, in the most successful of a series of séances requested by the grieving artist.

For Tissot to have resorted to spiritualism was not unusual or overly credulous in the 1880s, when it was a mainstream movement supported by intelligent individuals from all walks of society. In the face of scientific discoveries that increasingly pointed away from the existence of an all-powerful Christian deity directing individual destinies, the urge to prove the existence of the soul's life after the body's death became more pressing. Typically séances included such reassurances, and indeed during this appearance Newton's spirit made the longed-for pronouncement: "Peace, let it be. I love him still, and shall love him forever; the dead are not dead, but alive."[17]

Tissot's session with Eglinton occurred in London at the home of the artist Albert Besnard. Although another fellow artist, Jacques-Emile Blanche, later claimed that Eglinton was exposed as a fraud when "Kathleen" turned out to be a model who worked for Besnard, Tissot himself seems to have been convinced of the authenticity of the apparition.[18] The scene is described in an article illustrated by Besnard and published in 1888.[19] The entranced Eglinton toppled over onto his back while clouds of luminous smoke formed around him and eventually materialized into the form of a woman. Tissot cried out, "It is truly she!" Then, gradually recovering himself, he added, "I do not think that her chin was as small as that of this lady," and decided to record the features of the apparition. According to all accounts, Tissot then asked "Kathleen" to kiss him, which she did.[20]

The spirits appeared to hold some sort of glowing light source in their hands, the effect of which Tissot captures beautifully through the use of mezzotint, a printmaking technique favored for its capacity to create this sort of mysterious radiance. Nineteenth-century artists considered mezzotint "more suitable than any other style of engraving to represent phantasms, incantations, artificial lights and effects of night."[21] Unlike etching and drypoint, Tissot's other favorite techniques, mezzotint required the artist to work from dark to light. After roughing up the surface of a plate with a special tool known as a rocker—so that if it were printed at that stage the result would be a black rectangle—the artist polishes away areas to hold less ink and so print lighter; depending on the degree of smoothing out, the area appears more or less white, allowing the creation of mysterious and subtle tonal effects.

As a testament to his strong feeling for Newton, Tissot fetishized this "portrait," keeping the original oil with him in a room where he performed rituals.[22] Somewhat in contradiction to the extremely personal nature of the moment it depicts, however, the print circulated widely in three different colors. Was Tissot earnestly attempting to convert disbelievers to spiritualism, or merely indulging in sensationalism?

J.J. Tissot   *Apparition Médiunimique.*   Dark séance d'Eglinton du 20 May 1885 Londres.   no. 62

Parisiennes

After Tissot returned to Paris in 1882, he concentrated almost exclusively on images of French women, completing a series of fifteen pictures entitled *La Femme à Paris*. In the series Tissot set out to explore and celebrate a popular theme, the supposedly unique character of the women of Paris. First appearing in works of popular culture, such as the little pamphlets—known as *physiologies*—describing urban types (see fig. 29), the *Parisienne* was a personification of the city itself, a modern, attractive female hinting at mysterious gratifications for the urbane gentleman or male tourist. Repeated so often that it became an accepted fact, the notion that Parisian females were somehow a race apart, requiring categorization and interpretation, spurred countless representations of the figure in both high and low art. As one celebrant exulted, "Paris gives her in high degree the attractiveness, the delicacy, the coquetry, the magic seductiveness of certain hothouse flowers, specially cultivated for our hours of pleasure."[1]

Like the concept of a "New Yorker," the *Parisienne* was not a reality but an image—or rather a number of images, and so a logical choice for an artist seeking a theme for a series. Planning to follow up *La Femme à Paris* with a similar group on the theme of *L'Etrangère* (Foreign Woman), Tissot intended the pictures as a grand scheme to re-introduce himself to the Parisian art scene. Exhibited at the Sedelmeyer Gallery in Paris in 1885, *La Femme à Paris* also appeared a year later at the Arthur Tooth Gallery in London, under slightly different English titles (included here in parentheses), maintaining Tissot's British audience. By laying claim to intimate and detailed knowledge of the women of the city to which he had returned, Tissot presented himself as a true Parisian, still an insider after his years in a foreign country. Taking Parisian women as his topic was like taking Paris itself, since they personified the city—its variety, spectacle, entertainment, allure, and beauty. To endow his pictures with still more authenticity, the artist located his *Parisiennes* in various recognizable spaces, including the Bois de Boulogne, the Louvre, Versailles, and the Hippodrome.

fig. 29. "Brillante comme une étoile qui file," from Paul Perret, *La Parisienne*, 1868

Originally Tissot planned *La Femme à Paris* as a collaboration with prominent French authors, who were to write short stories based on the scenes depicted. The stories would then be published in conjunction with prints after the paintings. This part of the project was never completed, however, perhaps because the pictures received such negative critical reaction.

When first shown, the group of interrelated, large-scale canvases, exhibited in the English fashion under glass, created a collective impression of brightness, loud color, and modernity. Critics were puzzled by the odd mannerist elongation of the bodies and Tissot's looser, brushier style as he moved away from his former tightness of handling. Parisian reviewers frequently rejected the project as un-French: a common joke was that the figures were actually "*L'Anglaise à Paris*."[2] English writers too were disturbed by the exhibition, calling it a "popular picture show" and likening it to entertainment as opposed to art.[3]

63 *Le Journal* (*The Newspaper*), 1883
    Etching and drypoint, 14⅞ x 11⅝ in. (W. 73)
    Signed and dated in the plate, lower right
    Private collection

This print is after a pastel Tissot showed at the Palais de
l'Industrie in 1883 (Musée du Petit Palais, Paris). Women
reading newspapers were a common subject in nineteenth-
century French art. The modernity of the female reader was
equated with the up-to-the-minute, ephemeral quality of
newsprint. Strikingly different from Tissot's earlier etchings,
the work shows a new interest in stylization: moving away
from his former obsession with detail, he creates an overall
pattern of forms. Set against a flat background of horse-
chestnut leaves, the curve of the lady's bonnet across her
cheek, the countering line of the chair back, and her long
fingers holding the paper all suggest, rather than explicitly
depict, his fashionable subject.

   The rich velvety quality of Tissot's stumping, a technique
for which he was admired, is particularly evident here. His
printer Frederick Goulding used a Tissot print as an example
when explaining this technique to students.[4]

no. 63

64 *Berthe*, 1883

Etching and drypoint, 14$\frac{3}{16}$ x 11$\frac{1}{16}$ in. (W. 74)

Signed and dated in the plate, lower right; signed in pencil,
   lower margin, left; red monogram stamp, lower left

Private collection

When Tissot returned to Paris in the 1880s he again took up
portraiture, the genre that had established him in French
society in the first place. He worked mostly in pastel, a difficult but increasingly popular medium that he may have
taken up in emulation of Degas. He continued to make pastel
portraits even while hard at work on his biblical illustrations,
disproving the legend that he became an unworldly hermit
after his religious awakening. At one point he attempted to
combine the effects of pastel and etching by studying color
printmaking techniques. In 1890 Mary Cassatt wrote to her
fellow artist Berthe Morisot about an inspiring exhibition
of Japanese prints she had visited in Paris: "I saw Tissot
there who is also occupied with the problem of making
colored prints."[5]

Often, as in this case, he etched the portraits as well. Leaving the lower part of the plate unfinished, he concentrates on
the girl's face and beribboned bonnet. Shaded by the large
brim, her eyes have a knowing expression, created in part by
the white highlights in their centers. Yet despite her worldly
gaze and sophisticated costume, Berthe's figure suggests she
is still immature. Once we realize this, the affectation of her
fingers against her cheek seems more of an awkward attempt
at role-playing than an elegant pose.

no. 64

65 *L'Ambitieuse* (*Political Woman*), 1883–85
   Oil on canvas, 56 x 40 in.
   Signed, lower right
   Albright-Knox Art Gallery, Buffalo
   Gift of William M. Chase, 1909

In this work from the *Femme à Paris* series, a young lady in an elaborately ruffled pink gown, carrying a matching ostrich feather fan, with still more feathers in her upswept hair, enters a fashionable gathering on the arm of a white-haired man whose face is obscured. Several men in the foreground stare and whisper, whether in amusement at the couple's age difference or in speculation as to the mutual benefits of this odd match. Tissot underlines the excess of the lady's finery by the way her ruffles foam over the lower half of the canvas, spreading out over the nearby furniture as she passes. She is poised to sweep into the salon and overshadow—literally and figuratively—the seated lady in red in her path, from whom male admirers are distracted by the new arrival.

Above the heads of the couple is a clock in the shape of a lion with a woman's head, connecting this image to another painting in the *Femme à Paris* series entitled *The Sphinx*. In the upper right-hand corner is a bronze sculpture that appears to represent a man's severed head in the arms of a woman, perhaps John the Baptist and Salome or Judith and Holofernes. Like the sphinx, this detail suggests a recurring theme of the series, the mysterious power of women to captivate and dominate men. This young lady's "politics" are social not national, and the world she dominates is that of the ballroom not the legislature; through her abilities to clad herself fashionably and to comport herself well in the realm of diplomatic society, she hopes to raise her own position through that of her husband.[6]

In the background are a collection of individuals found in this sort of political gathering, including Turkish men in fezzes and other somewhat crude ethnic stereotypes such as the man with the hooked nose. An elderly lady with a formidable—and exposed—bosom represents a familiar figure of fun, the "mutton dressed as lamb." She peers through her spectacles at a man who in turn examines her through a lorgnette, suggesting the collective poor vision of the company. Political ambitions may be all-absorbing to them, but Tissot humorously reminds the viewer of the folly of it all.

The image of a woman entering a ballroom on the arm of an older man interested Tissot throughout his career; it appears in an early watercolor sketch entitled *A peine entrevue* and his oil painting *Evening*, exhibited at the Grosvenor Gallery in 1878.

The proposed author of the accompanying story for *L'Ambitieuse* was Jules Claretie.

no. 65

66 *Les Femmes de sport* (*The Amateur Circus*), 1883–85
   Oil on canvas, 58 x 40¼ in.
   Signed, lower left
   Museum of Fine Arts, Boston
   Juliana Cheney Edwards Collection

For this picture in the series Tissot chose a topical subject, a briefly popular type of circus in which aristocratic men took the place of professional acrobats for the entertainment of their peers. On the trapeze is Count Hubert de la Rochefoucauld performing at the Cirque Molier.[7] The *Parisiennes* in this case are the delighted women ogling the spectacle from the second tier of the audience. Many more women than men use binoculars or lorgnettes to appreciate the male forms on display, while the men in evening dress and top hats seem more preoccupied with each other than with the show.

The proliferation of hungrily gazing women suggests that Tissot believed this was typical of the Parisian female. His friend Edgar Degas had given him a sketch of a woman looking through field glasses, and this image clearly had particular meaning for the two of them. At a time when *voir* (to see) was a slang term for "to have sex with," the female looker was not an innocent image.[8] The reversal of customary roles, with women admiring semi-clad males, suggests that these *Parisiennes* are most likely demimondaines.[9] The woman in pink who stares out at us in amused interest reminds us that the women themselves are also on display.

The fatuous expression of the trapeze artist in the red leotard with its false pink "skin" is accentuated by his monocle; clearly, if he intended to perform any complicated routines he would have shed this fashionable accessory, but his performance appears to have been confined to merely perching above the ring and smiling. The clown gazing up at the ladies in the foreground wears a British flag on his costume, perhaps an attempt on Tissot's part to counter criticism that he had become too anglicized; since he is willing to suggest that the men of England are buffoons, he could hardly be mistaken for one of them.

Charles Yriarte, who had praised Tissot's work in the magazine *L'Art*, was chosen to write the accompanying story for this picture.

BUFFALO ONLY

no. 66

67 *La Demoiselle de magasin* (*The "Young Lady" of the Shop*), 1883–85
Oil on canvas, 58 x 39⅝ in.
Signed, lower right
Art Gallery of Ontario, Toronto
Gift from Corporations' Subscription Fund, 1968

Here the viewer becomes a customer in an establishment selling dress trimmings, lace, and ribbons. The young shop assistant politely holds open the door for us with one hand while she clutches our wrapped parcels in the other, ready to give them to the footman awaiting us outside. In the background is a busy street scene, identifiable as Paris by the red-and-white-striped awnings opposite.

Tissot's use of a raking perspective that tilts the space out toward the viewer is particularly effective here, emphasizing the exit enticingly created for us. It has been noted that this device reflects his interest in Japanese prints. By making the room appear almost as it would through a wide-angle lens, Tissot also plays with his audience's preconceived notions of the way vision itself functions.

As with all the *Femme à Paris* images, vision is at issue. The picture is composed around a series of gazes: that of the *demoiselle* at us, that of the man behind the door tipping his hat at the lady apparently engrossed in the merchandise, and that of the leering gentleman with the pince-nez who leans forward intently, exchanging looks with the shopgirl reaching toward an upper shelf. Tissot has included a visual pun; while this man peering in the window at first seems threatening, even sexually predatory, this is defused by the way the mannequin in the store obscures his torso. He becomes feminized, a figure of fun rather than the debonair ladies' man he fancies himself.

Fashion and shopping, both of which depended on visual consumption, had long been part of Parisian culture, although both intensified during the nineteenth century as architectural and technological changes affected customers and merchants alike. Large plate-glass store windows such as the one depicted here, gas lighting, mass-produced goods, and improved, widened streets all contributed to the emergent practice of combining an idle stroll with spending, particularly on the part of bourgeois wives eager to display their husbands' wealth.

Wearing a distinctive black uniform to convey elegance and sophistication to her customers, the shopgirl became a celebrated Parisian type. Often represented smartly stepping along with her bundle in the street as a *trottin* or delivery girl, she represented attractive femininity, the consumption of goods, and the new urban spaces in which the concept of the *Parisienne* was formed. The theme had long appealed to Tissot; he had sketched errand girls in the Paris streets as early as 1869.

The shop assistant was construed as a desirable and possibly available Parisian woman—one of the products on offer in the newly commercial atmosphere of the city. Tamar Garb has suggested that the counter leg carved into the shape of a monster curling out its tongue symbolizes a male version of the feminine practice of window shopping, which in French was called *leche vitrine* (licking the window); the salaciousness of this detail suggests the erotic "window shopping" of the top-hatted gentlemen in the streets, who admire the *demoiselles* rather than the merchandise.[10] More tamely, the tangled heap of ribbons spilling down the counter to form a heart shape on the floor hints at the emotion the shopgirl inspires.

The author chosen to write the story about *La Demoiselle de magasin* was Emile Zola, whose novel *Au bonheur des dames* (1883) had established him as a literary authority on women, shopping, and department stores.

no. 67

68 *La Demoiselle d'honneur* (*The Bridesmaid*), 1883–85
Oil on canvas, 50 x 40 in.
Signed, lower right
Leeds Museums and Galleries (City Art Gallery)

Wearing a stylish, brilliant blue dress, the bridesmaid stands out in a crowded Paris street. She captures the attention of all passers-by, including the groomsman attentively sheltering her from the drizzle while he helps her into a carriage; given the range of types staring at this figure, her power to attract the gaze seems to cut across class and gender lines. The pair of large red spectacles to the upper left is an optician's advertisement, emphasizing yet again the theme of vision that runs through *La Femme à Paris*.

The bridesmaid's costume is an important aspect of this *Parisienne*'s attraction. With its hourglass lines, a bustle enhanced by a strategically placed bow, short skirts, and tight-fitting bodice, such an outfit emphasized the female body in a way that was still novel; in the 1870s the outline of women's hips and legs had emerged for the first time since the early nineteenth century. Critics claimed that the new fashions were overtly sexual in the way they were molded to the body.[11]

No doubt Tissot chose to depict this fashionable garment from the side in order to portray the angle by which it was most recognizable. Discussing the shift in fashions since the time of hoopskirts, one French writer commented, "they dressed their hair and themselves as though they were always to be seen in profile—now the profile is an outline of a person who is not looking at us, who passes and could avoid us. The toilet has become an image of the rapid movement which bears the world onward, and which threatens to carry away even the guardians of our homes."[12] This new, figure-revealing dress was believed to allow women more freedom on the streets even as it attracted more attention. In contrast to the fashionable bridesmaid, the two shopgirls watching in envy and admiration wear practical, loose-fitting black uniforms. Resembling that of the assistant in *La Demoiselle de magasin* (no. 67), their garb protects them from such attentions as the lewd catcalls leveled at the bridesmaid by the errand boy in the foreground.

In the center of the canvas the hands of the two main characters engage in a subtle, charged dialogue. Revealing his haste in coming to the bridesmaid's assistance, the groomsman carries one glove in the hand holding the umbrella and has succeeded in pulling the other only halfway on or off. It is also unclear whether the bridesmaid is buttoning up or undoing her long elegant white gloves, through which peep enticing glimpses of pink flesh. The odd play of hands, so prominent and so suggestive, signals us to wonder what might be going to occur in the carriage.

The task of turning *La Demoiselle d'honneur* into a short story was assigned to François Coppée.

no. 68

69 *La Plus Jolie Femme de Paris* (*The Fashionable Beauty*), 1885
Etching and drypoint, 15¹³⁄₁₆ x 10 in. (W. 81)
Signed in the plate, lower left
Private collection

Tissot planned to issue etchings after all fifteen of his *Femme à Paris* paintings, but he completed only five and they remained unpublished. In this unusual composition the central woman appears to mesmerize a crowd of male admirers; accompanied by her chaperone, she proceeds through it effortlessly, creating a visible wake of reaction to her charm. Unlike the men, who turn to the side as if unable to withstand the intensity of her beauty, she presents herself frontally, her arms, neck, and head so symmetrical and poised that she resembles an icon. The short story inspired by this image was by Ludovic Halévy. It recounts how an unknown lawyer's wife became the toast of the city when favored by a wealthy prince, who delighted in demonstrating his social influence by decreeing a new "prettiest woman in Paris" every day. After a brief period of adulation, the young woman sinks into obscurity once again, having impoverished her husband by expensive purchases suitable to her new status.[13]

When the painting of *La Plus Jolie Femme de Paris* was exhibited, the catalogue noted that it depicted the "*monde d'affaires*, the world of the Bourse and banking house" rather than the high society of other images in the series. Tissot's eye for details of social class was acute, recording distinctions so subtle that they are lost to modern eyes. Differentiating the milieu of this work from that of *L'Ambitieuse* (no. 65), for example, is complicated by the fact that it appears to be set in the same ballroom or reception chamber, even including some of the same characters: the woman in the lower left foreground exposing her shoulders and arms, the man on the left with the slickly parted hair, and the long-faced gentleman with the monocle to the right. The works also share the theme of a woman rendering viewers powerless merely by silently appearing, a notion that clearly preoccupied the artist.

no. 69

70 *Ces dames des chars* (*The Ladies of the Cars*), 1885
   Etching and drypoint, 15¾ x 10 in. (W. 78)
   Signed in the plate, lower left
   Private collection

Three women race horse-drawn chariots around an indoor ring in a fashionable entertainment at the Hippodrome. With costumes vaguely reminiscent of classical armor, they wear tiaras resembling spiked rays of the sun and bodices embroidered with stars; the leading woman has a crescent moon on her crown. These celestial emblems endow the "ladies" with a mock-divine status, likening them to classical goddesses.

As the exhibition catalogue suggested when the painting of this subject appeared in London, this spectacle was the closest the present age could come to the glories of the ancient chariot races; yet here the performers were modern women who had their own particular appeal in French culture. A cult had grown up around the skilled or enthusiastic horsewoman, known as the "Amazon." The eroticism of the beautiful, frail female who restrains and directs the brute strength of a wild animal derived from the way this rhymed with the power of a woman to subdue a man. The idea of discipline, a crucial aspect of such dominant-submissive scenarios, is subtly suggested by the prominent whip carried by the leading charioteer, which stretches across much of the image and points to the rich and powerful men in the balcony.

The electric lights in the arching iron and glass architecture were an extremely modern feature that was thought to add to the artifice and illusion of a spectacle. The London exhibition catalogue commented, "if they are not beautiful, at all events under the glamour of electric light and amid the applause of the amphitheatre they seem so…Glamour is everything: the multitude applauds not what it sees but what it thinks it sees."

The author Tissot selected to write the story for *Ces dames des chars* was Théodore de Banville.

no. 70

71 *La Mystérieuse* (*The Mystery*), 1885
   Etching and drypoint, 15¹¹⁄₁₆ x 9¹⁵⁄₁₆ in. (W. 80)
   Signed in the plate, lower right
   Private collection

Like *La Plus Jolie Femme de Paris* (no. 69), the woman in this image is frontally posed, engaging the viewer directly as she proceeds toward us. The perspective of the alley, on either side of which are tall trees, enhances the peculiar elongation of her figure. Behind her marches a footman, clad like the man in *La Demoiselle de magasin* (no. 67), suggesting that she is perhaps the lady for whom the *demoiselle* holds the door in that picture. Visually closing off the alley is a nun holding a folding stool, who escorts an old lady. The odd juxtaposition of these characters with a fashionable woman walking her dogs contributes to the sense of mystery that Tissot once again wishes to create around the Parisian female.

When the oil version was exhibited in London, the catalogue asked, "What is her history? Is she a great lady? Who knows…It must remain a mystery whether she is going to keep a rendezvous…Is not this uncertainty, the sense of which crosses the mind 1,000 times a day as one meets people in the park or in the street, one of the piquant elements of life in a great capital?" More than idle narration of the picture, this question was a hallmark of modern urban life. Increasingly in the nineteenth century people lived in teeming cities where they were forced to share confined spaces with total strangers, a social situation almost entirely unknown to communities of older times.

Central to the idea of the *Parisienne* was the belief that she moved in a particular way, coordinated and graceful, conscious of a public spectator. Her fashionability, and particularly the attractiveness of her foot and leg, were key signifiers of her identity. "The *Parisienne* is as proud of her leg as a soldier of his sword. She knows well that it is an offensive weapon and that it produces sparks that bedazzle the eye of the passerby," commented one admirer.[14] To write a story inspired by *La Mystérieuse*, Tissot chose Henri Meilhac, co-author with Ludovic Halévy of *La Vie parisienne* (1866), an operetta that celebrated the women of the city.

no. 71

From Prodigal to Pilgrim

During the first half of his career, Tissot rarely demonstrated any interest in religious themes. His major ventures into this field were his depictions of the Prodigal Son: in 1863 he exhibited *The Return of the Prodigal Son*, set in the Middle Ages, together with a *Departure* in the style of the Venetian painter Carpaccio; and during his English period, he completed a popular series of paintings and engravings entitled *The Prodigal Son in Modern Life* (see nos. 72–75). Neither of these sets attempted to realize the biblical story with any degree of historical accuracy, and they were prompted by an interest in easily legible narrative painting rather than by piety.

In the middle of the 1880s, however, the artist's preoccupation with spiritualism solidified into a more traditional form of religious faith. Although he did not abandon all modern-life subjects from this point, until his death in 1902 he devoted most of his artistic energies to enormous projects of biblical illustration. In 1895 he exhibited his complete set of New Testament illustrations, 365 in all, in Paris. After their astounding success, he moved on to Old Testament subjects, ninety-five of which he showed in Paris in 1901.

This abrupt shift to a distinctly uncharacteristic type of subject matter may have been a tactical decision to exploit a new market. The artist did, after all, profit handsomely from the sale of reproduction rights, touring exhibition fees, and the purchase of his original watercolors by the Brooklyn Museum (New Testament) and by Jacob Schiff for the New York Public Library (Old Testament).[1] He had always been quick to alter his subject matter based on what he perceived as popular, as the French critics who accused him of plagiarism had noted at the outset of his career.

Yet Tissot may have been genuinely moved to produce his biblical illustrations. He claimed to have had a vision in the church of St. Sulpice in Paris, while making sketches for a painting in his *Femme à Paris* series (see nos. 63–71), in which he saw Christ comforting the poor; from this moment he knew that his calling was to record visions as they came to

him.[2] There are numerous accounts of his determination to produce truly inspired and inspirational religious art. According to one of the more dramatic stories, he destroyed his most recent devotional picture when a Parisian woman called it a masterpiece; by the third version of the work, the woman fell to her knees to pray, and Tissot was satisfied.[3]

As with his earlier works, Tissot worked from photographs as well as posed models. Reacting against the tradition of religious imagery that either idealized or modernized its subjects, he wished to make his own illustrations "authentic," true to the way things may have appeared in the actual days of the Bible. He traveled to the Middle East in 1885, 1889, and again in 1896. He went to Palestine, Egypt, Syria, and Lebanon to record the appearance of the landscape and people and to absorb inspiration from contact with the sites in which holy events had occurred. He was interested in isolating and recording modern "types" from the region, believing that physiognomies, fashions, and customs had not changed since biblical times. In the words of one commentator, "it was still the Unchanging East, and he saw the Arab Sheik dwelling in tents exactly like those his forefathers dwelled in four thousand years ago. He saw the same men and women leading the same life they had lived for tens of centuries."[4] Of course this idea, while occasionally and superficially accurate, was a strictly Western viewpoint; no country or civilization has ever remained the same for four thousand years. Yet Tissot firmly believed it was true, and it helped him paint "from life" as he had during his whole career.

Tissot had always been proficient in watercolor, having frequently resorted to it in studies for and replicas of his oils. Yet here he demonstrated a new fineness of handling, particularly in his use of gouache (watercolor mixed with white to make it opaque). His technique, combined with the novelty of his vision of the Bible, ensured the success of the series. Both the Old and New Testament sets toured extensively to Paris, London, and several cities in the United States. The British Prime Minister Gladstone wrote a letter of appreciation to Tissot, describing the New Testament as "a remarkable work by a remarkable man."[5] The press commented on their influence, claiming they had sparked religious revivals and that weeping, hysterical visitors moved through the exhibitions on their knees as if on a pilgrimage. The spectacular nature of the entertainment was enhanced by the addition of a magic-lantern slide show of some of the scenes, which accompanied the exhibition on its tour, at least in the United States.

Tissot's biblical illustrations, reproduced into the twentieth century in French and English editions of varying quality, were extremely influential. Not only did his conceptualizations of the characters and stories filter into children's Bibles and catechisms, they also had an impact on Hollywood. Though small in scale, his epic scenes and carefully researched costumes, with their much-promoted aura of authenticity, were imitated by filmmakers, including the Pathé brothers (*Passion*, 1912) and D. W. Griffith (*Intolerance*, 1916).[6] More recently, the makers of *Raiders of the Lost Ark* modeled the ark of the tabernacle on Tissot's reconstruction.

The Prodigal Son in Modern Life, 1881

In 1882, his last year in England, Tissot held a one-man exhibition at the Dudley Gallery, the lavishness of which indicated the prominence and wealth he had achieved. Liberty's of London decorated the space with gold-threaded tapestry wall-hangings, and vases of pampas grass and poppies contributed an exotic touch. The centerpiece of the exhibition was his series of paintings of *The Prodigal Son in Modern Life* (Musée des Beaux-Arts, Nantes), from which these prints were derived. Tissot was proud of both the paintings and the prints and continued to exhibit them, finally winning a gold medal for them at the Exposition Universelle in Paris in 1889.

The Prodigal Son had long been a popular subject for artists interested in creating narrative series. In his moralizing version of the story, Tissot echoed the ever-popular *Rake's Progress* of William Hogarth, much loved by the Victorians; indeed, the Rake himself follows the narrative of the Prodigal Son, although his story traces the consequences of not repenting in time.[7] Series such as these were particularly popular with English audiences. In pursuing the course of action from one image to the next they could "read" the work much as they followed serialized novels in magazines.

The theme of the Prodigal was clearly important to the artist, and speculation on his motivations in choosing it is tempting. In 1881, as a Roman Catholic living in sin with a divorced woman, Tissot would not have been able to partake of the sacraments and perhaps had occasional crises of conscience. This parable, with its implicit message of divine grace for those who may stray from God, may have comforted him with the thought that he too would be forgiven should he return to the "father."

Tissot may also have considered himself a Prodigal Son in the French art world and, hoping to be received with forgiveness, used these works to good advantage in reestablishing his career there. In 1881 he wrote a letter to the Hanover Gallery asking them to obtain a copy of the Salon catalogue, that he might look up addresses of prominent French artists in order to invite them to his exhibition; clearly he was attempting to increase his renown in his native country.[8]

Always the "dealer of genius," as John Singer Sargent snidely termed him,[9] Tissot was especially concerned about the dissemination of his *Prodigal Son* series. He decided to tap the American market by sending them to the dealer Knoedler in New York. "Without seeming too much to be acting for me please try to find out how the prodigal son is going. I have already sent [Knoedler] 25 proofs and I shall be interested to know whether these etchings have any chance of success," he wrote to another New York dealer.[10]

Tissot met the challenge of unifying the series through subtle compositional strategies. Each image contains a backdrop of water, in three cases clearly the Thames, and each has an architectural framework angled toward the rear left of the picture space.

He presented and dedicated this particular set of impressions to the famous French printer Delâtre, which suggests that he believed they were of superior quality.

72 *The Departure*
Etching, 12⁵⁄₁₆ x 14¾ in.
Second state, with text (W. 58, II/II)
Signed and dated in the plate, lower right;
    signed in pencil, lower left
Private collection

Luke 1: 11–12. *And he said. A certain man had two sons. And the younger of them said to his father, Father, give me the portion of goods that falleth to me. And he divided unto them his living.*

The Prodigal Son accepts a wallet and some serious advice from his elderly father. Underneath the table is a mother cat with several kittens, one of whom is straying away from the litter in a reference to the Prodigal's intentions. Similarly, one blossom falls from the vase of nasturtiums in the center of the table; the source of these flowers appears on the trellis in the family's country estate in the fourth image. In the background the father's other, more responsible son gazes out the window at the shipping on the river, daring only to dream about adventure.

Tissot subtly inserts religious references in an apparently simple contemporary vignette. Showing through the shades, the bars of the window behind the Prodigal take on the form of a cross. The model ship on the back wall, sporting the flag of the British merchant marine, not only suggests the father's trade but is also a symbol for the Church. Indeed, the father's house is an allegory for the true Church from which the son is wandering. Shells, with their symbolism of pilgrimage, had an additional, more personal meaning for Tissot, as his own father was a shell collector.[11]

A sister (or perhaps sister-in-law) looks up from her sewing. In a sketch for this work Tissot depicted Kathleen Newton in a Thames-side tavern window resembling those in works from the outset of his British career.[12] In this way he created a satisfying symmetry between the first and last pictures he exhibited in England.

73 *In Foreign Climes*
Etching, 12¼ x 14¹¹⁄₁₆ in.
Second state, with text (W. 59, II/II)
Signed and dated in the plate, lower left;
    signed in pencil, lower left
Private collection

Luke 1:13. *And not many days after the younger son gathered all together and took his journey into a far country, and there wasted his substance with riotous living.*

Tissot chose Japan as the distant land in which the Prodigal Son wastes his fortune, in part due to his interest in and knowledge of this country (see no. 10). As a non-Christian land, Japan also illustrated the Prodigal's deviation from God. Furthermore, middle-class Victorians tended to view the Japanese people as hedonistic, irresponsible, and un-ethical. The title character sits in a teahouse, toasting a line of Japanese fan dancers, who move to the sounds made by the singers and musicians. At the time such an image would have conveyed a strong sense of the exotic; as one British tourist to Japan wrote of a similar scene, "their forced gestures and extraordinary contortions harmonised little with our ideas of grace."[13]

Since such dancers and musicians were frequently sold into prostitution by their parents at a young age, and many teahouses functioned as brothels at night, Tissot clearly suggests the immoral lifestyle of his hero. Using an oblique term for a fallen woman, one reviewer called attention to the "frail female companion under his protection," who slumps against his shoulder as if worn out or inebriated.[14] With him is another Western gentleman, his blasé expression illustrat-ing his dissolution. Symbolically, the eerie light created by the floor-level lamps and the rice-paper lanterns contrasts with the natural light of the moon, struggling through the clouds in the background.

V. 11 And he said A certain man had two sons:
V. 12 And the younger of them said to his

Nº I
THE DEPARTURE

father, Father, give me the portion of
goods that falleth to me. And he divided
unto them his living.

no. 72

V. 13 And not many days after the younger
son gathered all together, and took his journey

Nº II
IN FOREIGN CLIMES

into a far country, and there wasted his
substance with riotous living.

no. 73

74 *The Return*
Etching, 12¼ x 14¾ in.
Second state, with text (W. 60, II/II)
Signed and dated in the plate, lower right;
   signed in pencil, lower left
Private collection

Luke 1:16–20. *And he would fain have filled his belly with the husks that the swine did eat: and no man gave unto him. And when he came to himself, he said, How many hired servants of my father's have bread enough and to spare, and I perish with hunger! I will arise and go to my father, and will say unto him, Father, I have sinned against heaven, and before thee. And he arose, and he came to his father. But when he was yet a great way off, his father saw him, and had compassion, and ran, and fell on his neck, and kissed him.*

The dock, shining with rain, resembles the polished wooden table on which the Prodigal sits in the first image, emphasizing the contrast between the two sites. Hungry and hopeless, he falls on his knees before his father in repentance, to find himself welcomed by an embrace so warmly enthusiastic that the old man's top-hat falls to the ground behind him. In the background men unload pigs and cattle from the ship on which the sinner has traveled, representing the swine that he has tended and also the animal condition to which he has fallen. The good brother looks on jealously, while his wife or sister touches her fingers to her face in a delicate gesture of amazement. The exaggeratedly tilted perspective in this image and the other designs in the series shows Tissot's favorite compositional technique borrowed from Japanese woodcuts.

75 *The Fatted Calf*
Etching, 12¼ x 14¹¹⁄₁₆ in.
Second state, with text (W. 61, II/II)
Signed and dated in the plate, lower left;
   signed in pencil, lower left
Private collection

Luke 1: 29–32. *And he answering said to his father, Lo, these many years do I serve thee, neither transgressed I at any time thy commandment: and yet thou never gavest me a kid, that I might make merry with my friends: But as soon as this thy son was come which hath devoured thy living with harlots, thou has killed for him the fatted calf. And he said unto him, Son, thou art ever with me, and all that I have is thine. It was meet that we should make merry and be glad for this thy brother was dead, and is alive again, and was lost, and is found.*

In the final scene, representing the generosity of God's grace, the newly returned Prodigal sharpens a knife in preparation for carving a roast under a silver platter at an outdoor dinner. His brother, striding up the stairs from a boat full of teammates in rowing costume, remonstrates angrily with the father, demanding to know why he, who has always behaved with honor, has been ignored while the spendthrift brother deserves a "fatted calf." His father gestures toward his recovered son and says that an errant soul has returned to the fold and must be shown the fullness of love and forgiveness.

Given the luxuriant trellis of nasturtiums in this work, and the symbolically isolated blossom on the table in the first image, Tissot implies that the fallen blossom has been restored to its source. If he indeed intended the series in part as a plea for renewed recognition in French art circles, the choice of this particular flower may not have been innocent. In the early 1870s, in search of a name for his coterie of like-minded artists, Degas had suggested *La Capucine* (The Nasturtium) after the Boulevard des Capucines, the location of their meeting and exhibition space in Paris. Perhaps Tissot was signaling a wish that his former avant-garde friends would once again embrace him.

V.16 And he would fain have filled his belly with the husks that the swine did eat: and no man gave unto him. V.17 And when he came to himself, he said, How many hired servants of my father's have bread enough and to spare, and I perish with hunger:

Nº III

THE RETURN

V.18 I will arise and go to my father, and will say unto him, Father, I have sinned against heaven, and before thee. V.20 And he arose, and came to his father. But when he was yet a great way off, his father saw him, and had compassion, and ran, and fell on his neck, and kissed him.

V.29 And he answering said to his father, Lo, these many years do I serve thee, neither transgressed I at any time thy commandment: and yet thou never gavest me a kid, that I might make merry with my friends: V.30 But as soon as this thy son was come which hath devoured

Nº IV

THE FATTED CALF

thy living with harlots, thou hast killed for him the fatted calf. V.31 And he said unto him, Son, thou art ever with me, and all that I have is thine. V.32 It was meet that we should make merry and be glad: for this thy brother was dead, and is alive again; and was lost, and is found.

The New Testament, 1886–1894

Tissot's New Testament was extremely popular and influential, although as a distinctly Roman Catholic interpretation it sparked some controversy among Protestants. When he came to America to promote the tour of the watercolors, he faced opposition from those predisposed to disagree with his interpretations. As one writer commented after meeting the supposedly divinely inspired artist, "he has the appearance of a provincial businessman in a Fedora hat somewhat too young for his years. His appearance and conversation bears out the matter-of-fact uninspired character of his work."[15] Particularly offensive to certain viewers was his rendering of the Passion scenes, with their emphasis on Christ's physical suffering. His depiction of Christ himself was also controversial. In the artist's opinion conventional representations had emasculated Christ by fearfully avoiding any vulgarly human characteristics. Believing in the importance of emphasizing Christ's embodiment as mortal man, he attempted to restore the vitality and substance he believed had been attributes of the real person.

Tissot wasted no opportunities to promote his Bible and resorted to such ploys as writing to individuals claiming there were only a few copies of the original edition remaining, and that he was personally notifying them of this opportunity rather than publicly announcing it.[16] In 1895 he sent the entire set of watercolors on a lengthy international tour to Paris, London, New York, Chicago, St. Louis, Philadelphia, and Omaha, among other places; and in 1900 a public subscription was taken up to purchase them for the Brooklyn Museum.

76 *Behold, he standeth behind our wall (frontispiece)*
Gouache, 5¹¹⁄₁₆ x 6¹⁵⁄₁₆ in.
Signed, lower left
Brooklyn Museum of Art
Purchased by Public Subscription

In this highly original composition, which served as the frontispiece to the illustrated Bible, Tissot combines several traditional symbols. Barely visible, Christ appears behind a grillwork, illustrating the Song of Solomon: "Behold, he standeth behind our wall, he looketh forth at the shadows showing himself through the lattice." In the foreground are several large sunflowers, symbolizing the Christian soul following Jesus, the sun. The vine and grapes that curve gracefully around the top and right side of the lattice also bear Christian connotations, representing the rite of the Eucharist. The message of this simple and delicate watercolor is that through the rituals of the true Church the worthy soul may find Christ.

Tissot had grown sunflowers in his English garden at a time when they had been the much-parodied symbol of the Aesthetic Movement; perhaps he found a certain satisfaction in endowing a formerly worldly plant with spiritual significance.

no. 76

77 *The Annunciation* (Luke 1:5–38)
   Gouache, 6⅝ x 8½ in.
   Signed, upper right
   Brooklyn Museum of Art
   Purchased by Public Subscription

The Virgin Mary hears from the archangel Gabriel that she will bear the Christ child. Clad entirely in white, Mary kneels in submission to the angel's word. The simplicity of her sleeping chamber, furnished only with carpets and pillows, was in Tissot's mind both archaeologically accurate and symbolic; like her white robe, it represents her great purity. As Gabriel speaks, Mary conceives—this is the moment at which Christ takes on human form.

In order to emphasize the historic and doctrinal significance of the scene, Tissot framed the illustration on the page with two knotted columns in an imitation of Byzantine manuscript illumination (fig. 30). Such columns frequently symbolized the Temple of Solomon.[17] With this detail Tissot may have been reminding the reader of the coming of the New Dispensation, as opposed to the law of the Old Testament, a common meaning of Annunciation images. Follow-

ing an established pictorial tradition, Mary is on the right and the angel on the left, perhaps to indicate the way to "read" the communication, from left to right as in a written text.

In painting the popular theme of the Annunciation, Tissot had numerous precedents to draw upon or refute. His most unusual contribution to the iconography of the scene was his vision of the angel, which he believed was an accurate interpretation of the biblical cherub, supposed to have three pairs of wings—one for veiling the face, one for covering the body, and one for flying.[18] More birdlike than human, he hovers on distinctively feathered blue wings that obscure his body, a pair of ambiguous extremities—hands or feet—dangling below. In an unusual interpretation of a halo, beams of light burst forth from a greenish face ringed with pink, creating a striking and peculiar color combination.

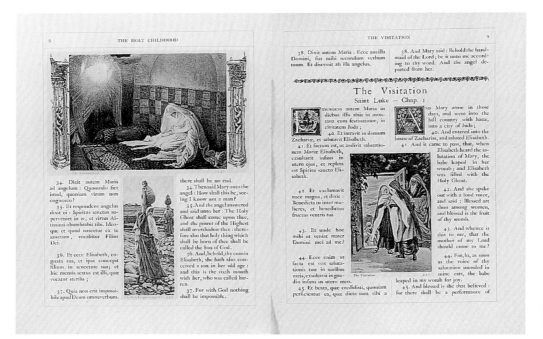

fig. 30. *The Life of Our Saviour Jesus Christ*, New York, 1899, vol. 1, pages 8–9

no. 77

78 *Jesus Teaching on the Sea Shore* (Mark 2:13–14)
Gouache, 10¾₆ x 7⁹⁄₁₆ in.
Signed, lower right
Brooklyn Museum of Art
Purchased by Public Subscription

79 *Jesus at Bethany* (Luke 10:38–42)
Gouache, 7⅞ x 11⅛ in.
Signed, lower left
Brooklyn Museum of Art
Purchased by Public Subscription

The most urgent aspect of Tissot's project was, as he viewed it, to present an incontrovertibly "true" Jesus. He maintained that his interpretation refuted various "modern travesties" of the image of Christ. He attempted to show him as both God and man, and as a Jewish man in particular. Here, by portraying Christ in the act of preaching to a diverse crowd, he puts to use his observation of the various types of people he saw on his trips to Palestine; according to Tissot himself, they include rich men from Tiberias, a modern town, Jews in black and white abayehs, Africans, women from Samaria, and Persian men.[19] Throughout the illustrations Christ is always in white, which both symbolizes his unstained nature and sets him apart from the disciples, who dress in earthier colors.

One reviewer singled out this work for commentary, noting "the natural grouping of simply curious or convinced followers and listeners" and appreciating the fact that Tissot had not idealized his subject: "Jesus preaching by the seaside sits on a pile of Oriental rugs spread on a boulder; his listeners are not well-dressed merchants but simple country folk."[20]

This vignette depicts Christ in the garden of Lazarus and his sisters Martha and Mary. Recognizable by her blue robe striped with green, yellow, and red, Mary Magdalene slumps in contemplation at his feet. Other followers listen attentively to his teachings, their intensity represented by the way they hold their heads.

Tissot's lifelong interest in compositional innovation is apparent in the odd tree trunk in the foreground, which divides the composition on its surface and effectively separates the men and the women. The tree may be a cedar, symbol of Christian incorruptibility. The garden is lush and decorative, full of olive trees and incongruous flowers found in English gardens rather than Middle Eastern ones, such as blue and pink delphiniums and orange day lilies. In the distance are white lilies and irises, signs of the Virgin Mary and of the reconciliation between God and man that Christ enacts. Perhaps the presence of English flowers in a supposedly "authentic" rendering of the Holy Land represents a longing on the artist's part for his lost garden in St. John's Wood.

no. 78

no. 79

80 *Mary Magdalene before her Conversion*
Gouache, 11 1/16 x 5 7/16 in.
Signed, lower left
Brooklyn Museum of Art
Purchased by Public Subscription

Like many nineteenth-century Christians, Tissot was fascinated by Mary Magdalene. He chose to illustrate numerous scenes in which she participated and invented this pair of "before and after" images. The theme of the sinful yet repentant female was endlessly compelling for his contemporaries, occurring in sermons, literature, writings on social reform, and frequently in paintings. In England fallen women were referred to as "Magdalenes," and Magdalenes' Homes took in prostitutes who wished to mend their ways. Although Bible scholars have argued that Mary Magdalene was neither a prostitute, nor the woman who wiped Christ's feet with ointment, nor the woman who listens to him in the garden of Bethany, Tissot accepted all of these identifications and illustrated them.

In the "before" picture Mary gazes seductively at the viewer in an attempt to corrupt him. In his commentary Tissot describes her living in sin with a Roman lover, full of pride and vanity, and points out that her red veil is the color of evil.[21] Decked with gold, jewels, cosmetics, and other signs of worldly vanity, she stands on a threshold, beckoning us to enjoy the pleasures of her lush garden, hinted at by the olives, lemons, and palm branches visible behind her.

81 *The Repentant Magdalene*
Gouache, 8 9/16 x 3 15/16 in.
Signed, lower left
Brooklyn Museum of Art
Purchased by Public Subscription

In his second image Tissot seems to imply that Mary need only step out of the garden to be in the spare stone courtyard that is the true path. Here the remorseful Mary gazes at a closed door; her desire to enter represents her wish to achieve the kingdom of heaven by leading a righteous life. Her hair streams down her back, a willing display of her shame, since loose hair was a sign of disgrace. The contrast between the decayed, decorated archway in the first watercolor and the solid, humble wooden door in the second suggests the difference between Mary's old and new lives. She is a symbol of true penitence, indicated by her devout expression and by what Tissot described as the dress of the lowest class, sandals and rags.[22]

Tissot had explored the theme of repentant femininity before, in his *Marguerite* series of the early 1860s (see no. 2). Moreover, as Norman Kleeblatt has pointed out, Mary resembles the artist's very own "Magdalene," the model and mistress from his English period, Kathleen Newton.[23]

no. 80

no. 81

82 *Mary Magdalene's Box of Very Precious Ointment* (Matthew 26:6–13)
Gouache, 8¹¹⁄₁₆ x 10¹⁵⁄₁₆ in.
Signed, lower right
Brooklyn Museum of Art
Purchased by Public Subscription

At the house of Simon in Bethany, Mary Magdalene is moved to anoint Christ's feet with medicinal ointment from an alabaster jar. This and her streaming hair were to become her attributes in religious art. As Tissot noted, Christ and the disciples are reclining in a space reserved for men alone, as was customary at this time, so Mary's intrusion is unexpected and unwelcome.[24] They react in alarm and anger that a valuable substance, reserved for funerals and worship, is wasted in this way. But Christ understands and forgives her gesture. Judas, identifiable by his red beard and hair and large nose cranes his neck to look on; in depicting him with this physiognomy, Tissot follows the tradition in Christian art responsible for creating the negative stereotype of the Jew. The yellow of his robe traditionally denoted deceit, cowardice, and jealousy.

The accumulation of busy patterns and details, besides being a hallmark of Tissot's style, is here harnessed to a pedagogical philosophy. Answering critics who accused him of excess, both in the number of images and the proliferation of details in each, Tissot argued that he wished "to take complete possession of the imagination of the spectator, to isolate him entirely from his preconceived ideas and to lead him slowly, yet without fatigue, along the paths where he will meet the true Christ."[25]

no. 82

83 *What Our Saviour Saw from the Cross*
Gouache, 9¹³⁄₁₆ x 9¹⁄₁₆ in.
Signed, lower right
Brooklyn Museum of Art
Purchased by Public Subscription

Of this image Tissot wrote: "this is the idea I wish to express …a momentary lull has occurred in the midst of the shouts and insults of the spectators, who are alarmed by the threatening signs in the sky and by the ever-increasing darkness."[26] In the gloom that has descended on the final moments of the life of Jesus, we are given a truly startling Christ's-eye-view of the scene at Golgotha. A great stillness has settled over the crowd, who are beginning to become uneasy at the celestial portents. In the bottom center of the composition are Christ's bloody feet, below which Mary Magdalene prays, her long hair streaming to the ground. St. John stands reverently to the left in a white robe, and the Virgin Mary also prays, with the two other Marys who traditionally accompany her at the cross.

The centurion in the red robe is likely the man who admits to Christ's divinity at the moment of his death, later referred to as Longinus. Three of the four soldiers who divided Christ's clothes among them sit on the periphery, one on the right still mocking. In the distance beyond the wall wait Christ's followers. Gaping wide to emphasize its significance, the tomb in which his body will shortly lie is a striking geometric shape amidst the organic forms.

Seeing a scene from the perspective of a character in its foreground is highly unusual in fine art, although it has become common in film. Here it places both the artist and the viewer literally in Christ's position, suggesting that through empathy with his sufferings one can understand the full significance of his death.

84   *The Dead Appear in the Temple*
(Matthew 27:50–54)
Gouache, 8⅜ x 11⅝ in.
Signed, lower right
Brooklyn Museum of Art
Purchased by Public Subscription

As Christ takes his last breath, the Babylonian tapestry in the doorway of the Temple of Herod is rent in two, representing the opening of Heaven to mankind now that Christ has died; simultaneously an earthquake occurs, and graves open to unloose the souls of the dead. Tissot's vision of this moment depicts ghostly rabbis haunting their earthly counterparts, disturbing the ceremony of the Paschal sacrifice; interrupted in the act of smearing blood on the great altar in a rite of symbolic regeneration, they flee out of fear of contact with the dead, which would render them unclean. Tissot carefully researched the complicated costume of the temple priests, which consisted of white linen robes bound with purple, blue, and red sashes wound around the torso (the robes represented earth and the sashes sea, air, and fire). The bands of the dead are coming unraveled, signifying their decaying state.

The location of the scene is in the innermost sanctuary of the Temple, where one encountered the presence of God and which only the high priests could enter. When Tissot attempted to render this authentically, he did so in accordance with Christian dogma as well as historical accuracy. He believed that the architecture of ancient temples symbolized their degeneracy. "In the midst of what I may call this superannuated decorative lumber, the noble simplicity of the personality and doctrine of Christ stands out all the more vividly," the artist declared, adding that Christ's role was "to sweep away…these mouldy accumulations."[27]

85   *The People, Beholding the Things that Were Done, Smote Their Breasts* (Luke 23:48)
Gouache, 11⁹⁄₁₆ x 7¹⁵⁄₁₆ in.
Signed, lower right
Brooklyn Museum of Art
Purchased by Public Subscription

In another portrayal of the events that occurred at the moment of Christ's death, Tissot illustrates the sky darkening violently in an eclipse. Upon witnessing this, the assembled crowds realize the error of their ways and recognize Jesus as the Son of God, returning home beating their breasts. Some hold their ears and shield their eyes in terror at the dreadful noise of the earth shuddering. The vertical composition, emphasized by the procession winding down from Golgotha, reaches its summit in the cross upon which Christ is hung. Under it remain the two Marys and St. John, demonstrating their faithfulness.

Upon his return from Palestine in 1887, Tissot showed the sketches and records of what he had seen to his father, who expressed great surprise at the way they deviated from his own ideas of what the Holy Land looked like: "'What! Is not Calvary after all a lofty sugar-loaf mountain, covered with rocks and brushwood?' 'Well, no,'" Tissot replied, "'Calvary, though it did occupy the summit of the town, was not more than from 20 to 22 feet high…Your error is very much that of most of the faithful. For a long time the imagination of the Christian world has been led astray by the fancies of artists.'"[28] Tissot hoped to employ his realist methods to correct such misconceptions, conveying a more accurate idea of the region and its people.

no. 84

no. 85

86 *Portrait of the Pilgrim* (*Self-Portrait*)
Gouache, 9¹⁄₁₆ x 5⅝ in.
Signed, lower right
Brooklyn Museum of Art
Gift of Thomas E. Kirby

Tissot placed this self-portrait on the final page of his illustrated New Testament. In the accompanying injunction, like a medieval writer concluding a holy text, he asks his readers to pray for him: "Ye who have read these volumes written for your benefit and have perhaps been moved by what they contain, as ye close them, say this prayer for their author: Oh God, have mercy on the soul of him who wrote this book, cause Thy light to shine upon him and grant to him eternal rest. Amen."[29]

He signed this request with a drawing of a scallop shell, a traditional symbol for the pilgrim, symbolizing his quest for religious and artistic truth as well as his actual travels to Palestine. Wearing the pillbox cap that appears in photographs of him at this time, he raises his hand in blessing over his readers. By depicting himself as a pilgrim, Tissot advertises his credentials as one who has been to the Holy Land and can therefore render it with authenticity, closing the book with an affidavit of its truth.

Yet this peculiar picture seems to be another type of self-portrait as well. The odd tableau in the foreground comprises objects of worship that may have come from Tissot's personal shrine, apparently arranged to represent both last rites and funeral practices. At a deathbed the priest would erect tapers and a makeshift altar covered by a white cloth in order to administer extreme unction; here Tissot seems to have set up his own version of such an arrangement, with a napkin-covered chair serving as an altar. On it are a crucifix, used during the rite, and a bouquet of violets, which in both traditional Christian and Victorian floral symbolism represent humility. On either side of the chair are long candles blowing in different directions, much the way the two "J's" of the artist's monogram mirror each other. In the foreground stands a vessel for holy water, also used in extreme unction.[30]

Tissot stands behind a catafalque, which is draped in a black pall with a white cross. Such coffin-like objects were displayed at requiem masses after a person had already been buried. There are four funeral wreaths, of the kind placed on graves, to the right of the image, and Tissot's monogram appears in a stylized representation of a wreath, perhaps meant to suggest stone-carving on a tomb. As the artist's hand passes over the pall it becomes transparent; he seems to hover in space, as though this were a portrait of his ghost rather than his living body, like the spirit of Kathleen Newton in *The Apparition* (no. 62).

By including the implements for his deathbed and funeral rites, Tissot provided viewers and readers images of objects with which they might mourn and pray for him. With his profound belief in the magical properties of images, perhaps he felt that even representations of the appropriate ritual paraphernalia could somehow assist in the salvation of his soul. Perhaps after an entire career spent in the attempt to make art replicate life, Tissot had begun to believe in his own creations.

no. 86

87 *Journey of the Magi* (Matthew 2:2), c. 1894
Oil on canvas, 27⅞ x 40 in.
Signed, lower left
The Minneapolis Institute of Arts
The William Hood Dunwoody Fund

This is one of a number of oil versions Tissot painted after his Bible illustrations. In his interpretation of the subject, the Magi are soothsayers and astronomers in the distinctive garb of their calling, yellow robes. Discovering a meteor or comet, they set out individually to follow what they recognize as a sign of the arrival of the Messiah. According to Tissot his picture represents the moment just after the caravans of the Magi join near Jerusalem. In the background are the volcanic hills near the Dead Sea, between Jericho, Jerusalem, and the Kedron Valley.[31] The three camels, symbols of humility and therefore of Christ, stride out in unison, reflecting the unified purpose of the three men. As representatives of other religions who are willing to pay homage to the infant Christ, their coming illustrates the supremacy of the true God.

Tissot's observation of the facial characteristics of contemporary Arabs and his careful use of brilliant, almost acid color in the capes, the scant patches of green, and the blue sky made this one of the strongest of his biblical images. One writer described the scene as "three desert sheiks of three distinct shades of brown, wearing cloaks of lemon, yellow, and orange, mounted on tall camels [forming] one of the most striking pictures as they advance up the sterile hill with their train winding far below in the turns of the rocky path."[32]

no. 87

The Old Testament, 1896–1902

"You can learn more about the Bible in half an hour from these pictures than by a year's study of the text…It is a living lesson, never to be forgotten," trumpeted the American Art Galleries in New York upon the opening of the exhibition of Tissot's Old Testament illustrations in 1904. In their eagerness to attract audiences and entrance fees, they neglected to mention that Tissot had died long before the series was completed, and that many of the illustrations were actually by his assistants. Perhaps this is why reviewers were more critical of the exhibition than they had been of the earlier, New Testament watercolors, detecting an unevenness and a heaviness of touch. The illustrations traveled widely, from Paris to London, Germany, and the United States, where they appeared in Chicago, Detroit, New York, and elsewhere. Once reproduced in book form, the work sold well; the twenty hand-printed copies of the "Imperial Memorial Edition" fetched as much as $5,000 each.[33]

In a letter to the American publisher of the New Testament, S. S. McClure, Tissot mentioned that he would be sending his French publisher Maurice de Brunhoff to New York in his place as he needed to stay behind to work on the illustrations for the Old Testament; he recommended de Brunhoff warmly, commenting on his integrity and his belief in the importance of their work. Since it was de Brunhoff who was largely responsible for marketing the entire set of Old Testament watercolors as by Tissot's own hand, he must in fact have been a rather unscrupulous businessman. Tissot maintained a mystical belief that Providence had chosen McClure, de Brunhoff, and himself for the project, and whether he himself was privy to any underhanded dealings is uncertain.[34]

With the Old Testament as well as the New, Tissot claimed that visions inspired his work. In a letter to McClure he described how "judges and kings appear before me as luminous as reality."[35]

fig. 31. "M. Tissot and His Guide," from *McClure's Magazine*, March 1899

no. 88

88 *Building the Ark* (Genesis 6:14)
Gouache, 8$\frac{7}{16}$ x 11$\frac{5}{16}$ in.
Signed, lower right
The Jewish Museum, New York
Gift of the heirs of Jacob Schiff

Dismayed with the evil thoughts and behavior of mankind, God decides to destroy his creation. The only people to be spared are the righteous Noah and his family. Instructing Noah to build an enormous ark and to collect a pair of every animal, God floods the earth, killing all living creatures. Noah's ark sails for a year and eleven days before the waters recede.

Tissot depicts Noah, on the left with his three sons Shem, Ham, and Japheth, in the process of obediently assembling the ark. While Noah and one son examine wooden rods for strength, another son hoists a beam up a makeshift ramp. The gentle curve of the board over his shoulder parallels the curve of the plank up which he walks, a compositional device that unifies the composition. Tissot's handling of the man's arm and shoulder creates a sense of the weight of the load. To the right the son with the full beard and head of hair typifies

Tissot's vision of the way people looked in biblical times. Photographs found after his death reveal that he posed models in his studio wearing enormous fake beards and wigs.[36]

The ark was an important subject for more than its picturesque qualities. In Christian symbolism the vessel built at God's command stands for the Church: it contains both saints (represented by the peaceable animals) and sinners (the predators), and it may face opposition but is never overturned. Only by passing through danger can the faithful find salvation, much as Noah trusts in God and is saved. The ark riding the flood is also seen as a prefiguration of the sacrament of baptism. In other words, Noah and his sons are depicted in the sacred act of carrying out God's will.

BUFFALO ONLY

89 *Hagar and the Angel in the Desert* (Genesis 16:7)
Gouache, 9⁷⁄₁₆ x 6 in.
Signed, lower left
The Jewish Museum, New York
Gift of the heirs of Jacob Schiff

Realizing she is barren, Abraham's wife Sarah asks him to father a child with her Egyptian maid, Hagar. When Hagar becomes pregnant, Sarah fears for her own status in Abraham's eyes and treats the maid badly. Hagar flees into the desert to escape, and God sends an angel to comfort her as she rests at a well. Telling Hagar to return to her mistress and submit obediently, the angel reassures her that she will bear a son, to be called Ishmael.

Tissot depicts Hagar pausing on the brink of the well in the act of pulling up a jug of water, as if startled by the first words of the angel. Though somewhat androgynous, this proud angel is very different from the one who appears to Mary in Tissot's Annunciation scene (no. 77). Tissot studied theological opinions about angels and carefully differentiated between the various hosts. Despite his age the artist's powers of observation were still acute, and he renders tiny details such as the curve of Hagar's toes with great delicacy.

The present scene foreshadows a later moment in Hagar's life, when she and her son Ishmael (who has displeased Sarah by mocking the child she eventually bore, Isaac) are sent a second time into the desert to perish of thirst. Once again the Lord sends an angel, who leads her to a well.

BUFFALO ONLY

no. 89

90 *Rebecca Meets Isaac by the Way* (Genesis 24:65)
Gouache, 11⅝ x 7⁷⁄₁₆ in.
Signed, lower right
The Jewish Museum, New York
Gift of the heirs of Jacob Schiff

In search of a wife for his master's son Isaac, Abraham's
servant prays to God to send him a suitable woman; he asks
that he should be able to recognize her when she offers him
and his camels water at a well. Having traveled a great distance to Mesopotamia from his master's home in Canaan, the
servant encounters Rebecca, a beautiful young woman who
proffers the appropriate hospitality. She bravely accepts the
offer of marriage to Isaac, sight unseen, and travels to her
future husband's family. As she nears the end of her journey,
she unexpectedly encounters Isaac meditating in the fields.
He looks up at the approaching camel train and they see
each other, neither knowing the other's identity. Although
Rebecca's retinue of retainers and servants suggests the
wealth Isaac will gain through the marriage, his modesty is
clear from the way in which he greets her, gazing up from
the humble back of a donkey.

In this carefully composed image Tissot explores the play
of bright color and surface pattern, rhyming the donkey's
lazily flattened ears with the broad blue and white bands
holding together the caravans. The artist knew from firsthand experience what riding a donkey was like, as he occasionally traveled in this manner during his sojourn in the
Holy Land. An illustration in an American magazine shows
him riding up the Mount of Olives from the town of Bethany
(fig. 31).

YALE AND QUEBEC ONLY

no. 90

no. 91

91 *Joseph Reveals His Dream to His Brethren* (Genesis 37:8)
Gouache, 8⅞ x 12⁷⁄₁₆ in.
Signed, lower right
The Jewish Museum, New York
Gift of the heirs of Jacob Schiff

Joseph, youngest son of Jacob and Rachel, and grandson of Isaac, relates two dreams that foretell his future eminence. In the first, he and his ten brothers are binding sheaves of wheat when his own bundle stands upright of its own accord, and the sheaves of the other brothers gather round to pay homage. In the other, the sun, moon, and eleven stars bow down to him, symbolizing the obeisance of his father, mother, and brothers (including his full brother Benjamin). Incensed by the idea that Joseph, the youngest and favorite son of Jacob, should have power over them, and jealous that their father should have given him the coat of many colors, the brothers conspire to be rid of him. They throw him into a pit, take his coat, and stain it with goat's blood to convince Jacob that his favorite son is dead. In reality a slavetrader has picked Joseph up to sell into slavery in Egypt.

In Tissot's watercolor the brothers display a range of reactions to Joseph's announcements, from boredom to anxiety; two are even fast asleep on the bank on the left. Joseph's position, literally above his brothers, symbolizes his future rise to leadership. Later in Tissot's Bible he appears sitting high on an Egyptian throne to receive those who had once forsaken him. Like many Christians of his time, Tissot viewed events in the Old Testament as a prefiguration of those in the New, in which light Joseph's poor treatment at the hands of his own kin looks forward to Christ's betrayal by Judas. Despite his extreme youth, suggested by his boyish pose with one leg tucked up beside him, Joseph conveys dignity with the gesture of teaching used in Tissot's New Testament watercolors by Christ; similarly, his brothers (from whom will spring the twelve tribes of Israel) resemble the twelve Apostles.

BUFFALO ONLY

no. 92

92 *Joseph Dwelleth in Egypt* (Genesis 50:22)
Gouache, 9 1/16 x 10 7/8 in.
Signed, upper right
The Jewish Museum, New York
Gift of the heirs of Jacob Schiff

Sold into slavery in Egypt, Joseph serves in the house of Potiphar. After being thrown into jail when wrongfully accused by Potiphar's wife of insulting her, he triumphs over adversity when his skill at interpreting dreams comes to the attention of the Pharaoh. After reading Pharaoh's dream of fat and lean cattle as a portent of poor harvests, Joseph advises that food be stored in preparation; his prediction averts famine, and Pharaoh rewards him by making him a vizier, a high official. His transformation is so complete that his brothers do not recognize him when they come to Egypt to beg for food; ultimately Joseph reveals his identity and forgives them.

In the tradition of artist-explorers such as David Roberts and William Holman Hunt, Tissot recreated ancient Egypt with a mixture of fantasy and archaeological accuracy. Although he renders the forms of columns of the classical Egyptian period accurately, for example, he arranges them in a way that was largely his own invention. The decorations on the standards carried by the Egyptians paying homage to Joseph—a sun beetle, a vulture goddess, a solar disk with wings, and the head of another goddess—are also an embellishment of Tissot's, although the emblems themselves are based on known artifacts.[37] This colorful realization of ancient Egypt was popular, and set designers drew on Tissot's illustrations in the staging of a play about Joseph that was performed in New York in 1912 and London in 1913.[38]

In Christian doctrine Joseph's descent into the pit and his subsequent elevation were prefigurations of Christ's death and resurrection, the subtext of this image. The bowing Egyptians prefigure the followers of Christ, and the sunflower fan in the foreground may represent the Christian soul (see no. 76).

YALE AND QUEBEC ONLY

no. 93

93 *The Plague of Locusts* (Exodus 10:13)
Gouache, 7¾ x 9⅜ in.
Signed, lower right
The Jewish Museum, New York
Gift of the heirs of Jacob Schiff

In Exodus God sends a series of ten plagues upon Egypt in order to compel Pharaoh to release the Israelites from slavery. Locusts are the eighth plague, destroying precious crops as they devour all vegetation in their path. (The other plagues are water turning into blood, frogs, gnats, flies, cattle disease, boils, hail, darkness, and the death of the firstborn.) Tissot shows Moses summoning the east wind, which will bring the locusts, by extending his staff over a strangely sterile and uninhabited Cairo. Here Tissot's vision of ancient Egypt is less archaeological than decorative; clearly his main aim is to create a striking composition of stark geometric forms. On the horizon the three enormous pyramids of Giza tower over the city. The brooding sky prefigures the effect of the swarming locusts, which were to be so dense that "they covered the face of the whole earth, so that the land was darkened."

The devastation temporarily weakens Pharaoh's resolve, and he begs forgiveness of Moses, only to refuse again to let the Israelites go once the plague is over.

YALE AND QUEBEC ONLY

Notes

The Painter of Modern Love

1 *Baudelaire: Selected Writings on Art and Artists*, trans. with an Introduction by P. E. Charvet (Harmondsworth: Penguin, 1972), 390–435.

2 Ibid., 391.

3 For a discussion of Tissot, femininity, and the reproducible dress, see Nancy Rose Marshall, "'Transcripts of Modern Life': The London Paintings of James Tissot, 1871–1882," Ph.D. diss., Yale University, 1998, 124 ff.

4 See Michael Wentworth, *James Tissot* (Oxford: Clarendon Press, 1984), 88, 108.

5 On the implications of Tissot's garden scenes, see Nancy Rose Marshall, "Image or Identity: Kathleen Newton and the London Pictures of James Tissot," in Katherine Lochnan, ed., *Seductive Surfaces: The Art of Tissot*, Studies in British Art 6 (New Haven and London: Yale University Press, 1999).

6 The friend was Edmond de Goncourt; see Wentworth, 1984, 7.

7 See Tamar Garb, "Painting the 'Parisienne': James Tissot and the Making of Modern Woman," in Lochnan.

8 *The Life of Our Saviour Jesus Christ* (New York, 1899), "Introduction," 1:ix.

9 See Wentworth, 1984, 187.

Costume Pieces

1 The most complete accounts of his life are by Willard Misfeldt, "James Jacques Joseph Tissot: A Bio-Critical Study," Ph.D. diss., Washington University (Ann Arbor, Michigan: University Microfilms International, 1971), and Wentworth, 1984; the following information is distilled from their research.

2 Wentworth, 1984, 35.

3 Thanks to Carlos Eire for his insights into representations of Luther.

4 Thanks to Walter Cahn for verifying this identification.

5 Louis Lagrange, *Gazette des Beaux-Arts* 10 (1861): 346.

6 Charles Clément, *Journal des débats*, May 25, 1870, 2.

7 *Athenaeum*, June 11, 1870, 779.

8 *Illustrated London News*, July 17, 1880, 54.

9 *Times*, May 21, 1872, 7.

10 Dickens described the Thames-side tavern "The Six Jolly Fellowship Porters" in his novel *Our Mutual Friend* (1865): "Externally, it was a narrow lopsided wooden jumble of corpulent windows heaped one upon another as you might heap as many toppling oranges, with a crazy wooden verandah impending over the water" ([London: Penguin, 1985], 104).

11 "His peculiar gifts have made him preeminently a waterside painter; and just as Mr. Whistler, in his etchings, may be classed as the Claude of Old Chelsea, and the Cuyp of Rotherhithe; so may we qualify Mr. Tissot as the Watteau of Wapping and the Hogarth of Horsleydown" (*Daily Telegraph*, May 21, 1874, 7).

12 Thanks to David Barquist for identifications of furniture and decorative objects in this entry and elsewhere.

13 Michael Wentworth, *James Tissot: Catalogue Raisonné of His Prints* (Minneapolis: Minneapolis Institute of Arts, and Williamstown, Massachusetts: Sterling and Francine Clark Art Institute, 1978), 146.

La Vie moderne

1 In 1876 the framer and dealer Alphonse Thibaudeau in London recorded rebinding books by these authors for Tissot. Unpublished ledger, Special Collections, Getty Center Library.

2 Misfeldt, 1971, 66.

3 Théodore Thoré, *Salons de W. Bürger* (Paris, 1870), 2:101.

4 Charles Clément, *Journal des débats*, May 13, 1864, 2.

5 For more on Tissot's fashions, see Edward Maeder, "Decent Exposure: Status, Excess, the World of Haute Couture, and James Tissot," in Lochnan.

6 Lou Taylor, *Mourning Dress: A Costume and Social History* (London: Allen and Unwin, 1983), 66.

7 Anon., *Manners of the Aristocracy by One of Themselves* (London, no date), 85.

8 Elie Roy, *L'Artiste*, July 1, 1869, 81.

9 *Fables of La Fontaine*, trans. Elizur Wright, Jr. (Boston, 1841), 242–43:
"About one month thus mourned the fair;
Another month, her weeds arranged;
Each day some robe or lace she changed,
'Til mourning dresses served to grace
And took of ornament the place."

10 William A. Coles, *Alfred Stevens* (Ann Arbor: University of Michigan Museum of Art, 1977) suggests that this image is meant to refer to a line in La Fontaine's fable: "The whole flock of cupids returns to the dovecote" (49).

11 Wentworth, 1984, 66.

12 Thanks to Mimi Yiengpruksawan for her identification of the Asian objects.

13 Roy, 81.

14 Ibid.

15 Thomas Gibson Bowles, *The Defence of Paris Narrated As It Was Seen* (London, 1871), 30.

16 See Misfeldt, 1971, 113–19, and Wentworth, 1984, 80–83.

17 Bowles, 1871, 155.

18 Willard Misfeldt, *J. J. Tissot. Prints from the Gotlieb Collection* (Alexandria, Virginia: Arts International, 1991), 54.

19 Bowles, 1871, 151.

20 Ibid., 158.

21 Misfeldt, 1991, 70.

22 Bowles, 1871, 336.

23 Wentworth, 1978, 26–27.

Men of the Age

1 Theodore Reff, *Degas: The Artist's Mind* (New York: Harper and Row, 1976), 101.

2 Krystyna Matyjaszkiewicz, ed., *James Tissot* (London: Phaidon Press and Barbican Art Gallery, 1984), 104. She suggests that Tissot must have made a special visit to London in 1869 or 1870 in order to paint this portrait. Burnaby came up with the title for the magazine as well as capital.

3 Burnaby wrote *A Ride to Khiva* (1876), *On Horseback through Asia Minor* (1877), and *A Ride across the Channel* (1882).

4 John Collier, *Manual of Oil Painting* (London, 1880), 48.

5 "Purchase was contrived in order to keep military rank and emolument in the hands of the upper classes," wrote one angry soldier (Anon., *The Army, the Horse-Guards, and the People* [London, 1860], 23).

6 *Beeton's Manners of Polite Society* (London, 1876), 31.

7 Burnaby was apparently so pale that he powdered his beard stubble to harmonize with the rest of his complexion (J. Redding Ware and R. K. Mann, *The Life and Times of Colonel Fred Burnaby* [London, 1885], 338. In Tissot's painting there is a white highlight along his chin that might hint at this cosmetic.

8 David Harvey, *Consciousness and Urban Experience: Studies in the History and Theory of Capitalist Urbanization* (Baltimore: Johns Hopkins University Press, 1985), 6.

9 Details of Marsden's financial troubles are taken from bankruptcy reports in *The Times,* August 24, 1881, 12; September 9, 1881, 10; August 31, 1882, 9; October 14, 1881, 10; September 14, 1887, 13; January 25, 1888; 12; January 3, 1901, 13; January 30, 1901, 5.

On the Thames

1 Jane Abdy, "Tissot: His London Friends and Visitors," in Matyjaszkiewicz, 1984, 40–52.

2 Thanks to John House for bringing this aspect of Tissot's technique to my attention.

3 The painter Louise Jopling recounted a trip taken with Tissot in 1873, after he had invited her and her sister Alice "to come and spend the day at Greenwich, where he was painting his charming pictures of scenes by the river Thames. I was to bring my sketching materials" (*Twenty Years of My Life* [London: John Lane, 1925], quoted in Misfeldt, 1971, 133).

4 *Times*, May 22, 1876, 6.

5 *Saturday Review*, May 27, 1876, 683.

6 On the other hand, some city dwellers, Tissot among them, reveled in the smog as a sign of urban vitality. Edmond de Goncourt noted in his journal that Tissot had told him that he liked London's odor of coal because it smacked of the "battle of life" (Goncourt, *Journal* 3: 174, quoted in Wentworth, 1984, 132).

7 W. S. Lindsay, *Manning the Royal Navy and Mercantile Marine* (London, 1877), 41–43. Despite the fact that the man is not in full naval uniform, reviewers saw him as a Navy man.

8 *Graphic*, May 13, 1876, 471.

9 Traditionally the Trafalgar was chosen by the Liberals, the Ship or the Crown and Sceptre by the Tories. (Anon., *An Anecdotal History of the British Parliament* [London, 1880], 451).

10 Thomas Gibson Bowles, *Flotsam and Jetsam* (London, 1882), 32.

City Life

1 *Echo*, May 1, 1874, 2.

2 *Times*, May 2, 1874, 12.

3 See *Ten Letters from a Bluecoat Boy* (London: Alfred W. Bennett, undated), 14–15. The author suggested that the sleeping arrangements in the wards be rearranged to allow for monitoring.

4 *Athenaeum*, May 30, 1874, 738.

5 Anon., *Etiquette for Ladies and Gentlemen* (London, 1874), 69.

6 *Spectator*, May 30, 1874, 692.

7 *Athenaeum*, November 1, 1879, 568.

8 Augustus C. Hare, *Walks in London* (London, 1878), 2:139. Other writers complained about their "tawdriness, hastiness, sketchiness, and show" and their "violent digressions from true taste." See Donald J. Olsen, *The Growth of Victorian London* (New York: Penguin, 1976), 48, 50.

9 "The barrel organ is the opera of the street-folk…I cannot call to mind any scene on our many journeys through London that struck the authors of this pilgrimage more forcibly than the waking up of a dull, woe-begone alley, to the sound of an organ. The women leaning out of the windows—pleasurably stirred, for an instant, in that long disease, their life—and the children trooping and dancing around the swarthy player" (*London: A Pilgrimage* [London, 1872], 175–76).

10 *Street Music in the Metropolis* (London, 1864), 2–3, 105. The petition was signed by, among others, Alfred Tennyson, Charles Dickens, John Everett Millais, Thomas Carlyle, William Powell Frith, Thomas Faed, John Phillips, Alfred Elmore, John Callcott Horsley, Wilkie Collins, William Holman Hunt, John Leech, John Herbert, James Sant, Francis Grant, Thomas Woolner, and Seymour Haden (41–42).

11 Ibid., 13–16.

12 Caroline Arscott reads Tissot's outsider figures as stand-ins for the artist himself; she calls attention to the elaborate embroidery on the organ's cover as a sign for original art-making, in contradistinction to the perception of the organ grinder as a mere mechanical laborer ("The Invisible and the Blind in Tissot's Social Recitals," in Lochnan).

On Shipboard

1 Bowles, 1882, 59 (written in 1874).

2 *Berthe Morisot's Correspondence*, ed. Denis Rouart and trans. Betty W. Hubbard (London: Camden, 1986), 105.

3 *Tablet*, June 27, 1874, 810.

4 *Modern Painters*, V, in *The Works of John Ruskin*, ed. Alexander Cook and Edward Wedderburn (London, 1903–11), 7:353. Ruskin famously summarized Tissot's work at the Grosvenor Gallery in 1877 as "mere coloured photographs of vulgar society." "Fors Clavigera," Letter 79, July 1877, in *Works* 29:161.

5 *Tablet*, June 27, 1874, 810.

6 *Athenaeum*, May 30, 1874, 736.

7 *Graphic*, August 18, 1877, 150; with engraving.

8 *Spectator*, May 26, 1877, 665.

9 George Rhead, *History of the Fan* (London, 1910), 137.

10 Teddy Archibald, private communication, October 19, 1995.

11 *Supplement*, August 18, 1877, after page 168.

12 In the novel Nigel Beauchamp vacillates between two eligible ladies for his wife: "Cecily…was England, and Renée holiday France" ([Oxford: Oxford University Press, 1988], 314).

13 Francis E. Hyde, *Cunard and the North Atlantic* (London: Macmillan, 1975), 62.

14 From *American Notes*, in F. Lawrence Babcock, *Spanning the Atlantic* (New York: Knopf, 1931), 60.

Social Graces

1 The French art critic and recorder of society Edmond de Goncourt recounted being told "that Tissot, that plagiarist painter, had great success in England. He had the idea, the ingenious exploiter of English folly, to have a studio outside of which is an antechamber where one finds, at all times, champagne at the disposal of visitors and around the studio a garden where one sees, all day long, a servant in silk stockings scrubbing and polishing the leaves of the bushes" (*Journal*, November 3, 1874, 2:1001–2).

2 *Degas Letters*, ed. Marcel Guérin, trans. Marguerite Kay (Oxford: Cassirer, 1947), 11–12, 30, 33.

3 Unpublished letter to unidentified recipient, October 2, 1879, Getty Center Library.

4 Michael Wentworth discusses the various conflicting stories about Tissot's involvement with the Commune, concluding that it was indeed possible that he did take part in it in some way, if only to prevent the confiscation of his home. He cites the artist Jacques-Emile Blanche as the source of the rumor that Tissot was motivated out of concern for his belongings (1984, 80–83). Willard Misfeldt argues that it is unlikely Tissot participated in the Commune and that rather he was the victim of mistaken identity (1971, 113–19).

5 *World*, May 26, 1875, 12.

6 Charles Baudelaire, "The Painter of Modern Life," in *The Painter of Modern Life and Other Essays*, ed. and trans. Jonathan Mayne (London: Phaidon, 1964), 40; 1–4.

7 Christopher Wood, *Tissot: The Life and Work of Jacques Joseph Tissot, 1836–1902* (Boston: Little, Brown, 1986), 71.

8 Unpublished letter to Mr. Pyke, October 11, 1878. Getty Center Library.

9 *L'Art* 3 (1875): 255. The *Times* critic identified the violinist as Madame Norman-Neruda, giving a private concert in a "West-end music-room" (May 29, 1875, 6). A letter from Oliver Brown of the Leicester Gallery to Lawrence Howard at the Manchester City Art Gallery, dated June 30, 1933, recognized Tissot's friends Heilbuth, Bowles, and de Nittis, agreed with the identification of Benedict and de Soria, and added the following sometimes conflicting identifications: he believed that the violinist was Mlle. Diaz de Soria, the bearded man in the doorway to the left Frederic Leighton, and the large man seated on the staircase the Marquess of Lorne (Manchester City Art Gallery Files). Other identifications include the painters John Callcott Horsley and Sir Francis Grant as the two white-bearded men in the doorway and, alternatively, Lord Portman as the large man on the staircase (J. A. Fuller, letter to Lawrence Howard, May 16, 1934, Manchester City Art Gallery Files). The woman in profile on the right has been seen as a younger Queen Victoria, who would have been fifty-six in 1875 (Harry MacDonald, letter of

October 2, 1991, Manchester City Art Gallery Files). James Laver recorded that the house was that of a family called Coope (*Vulgar Society: The Romantic Career of James Tissot* [London: Constable, 1936], 33–34). Possibly he was referring to Octavius Edward Coope, who had made his money in breweries and in 1874 became MP for Middlesex (*Licensed Victuallers' Yearbook* [London, 1876], 80–81). He lived at 41 Upper Brook Street, London (*Court Directory*, 1872).

10 Richard Ormond notes, "to qualify as a *Vanity Fair* caricaturist was not unlike entering society itself. The essential requirement was to be already socially acceptable; to be foreign as well was a distinct advantage" (*Vanity Fair* [London: National Portrait Gallery, 1976], 8).

11 *Saturday Review*, June 12, 1875, 756–57.

12 Quoted, for instance, in G. Ashdown Audsley, *Catalogue of a Loan Collection of Fans at the Liverpool Art Club* (Liverpool, 1877), v.

In the Garden

1 Mrs. J. Francis Foster, *On the Art Of Gardening* (London, 1881), 3.

2 Earl of Ilchester, *Chronicles of Holland House, 1820–1900* (London: John Murray, 1937), 435.

3 Princess Marie Liechtenstein, *Holland House*, 2 vols. (London, 1874).

4 Peter Bailey, *Leisure and Class in Victorian England* (London: Routledge and Kegan Paul, 1978), 125–27.

5 Wood, 101.

6 As one enthusiast of the sport asked, "in these latter days have not cricket and other contemporaneous sports had something to do in forming the physique and muscle of the men who fought in the Crimea and India, or who stamped out the embers of mutiny?" (Charles Box, *The English Game of Cricket* [London, 1877], 1); another commentator simply declared, "[cricket] is a healthy and a manly sport; it trains and disciplines the noblest faculties in the body, and tends to make Englishmen what they are—the masters of the world" (anonymous writer in *Temple Bar*, quoted in Box, 80).

7 Max Schulz discusses the mixture of physical and spiritual love associated with gardens in his *Paradise Preserved: Recreations of Eden in Eighteenth and Nineteenth-Century England* (Cambridge: Cambridge University Press, 1985), 251–77. See also Susan Casteras's discussion of the garden in courtship imagery in "'Of Queen's Gardens' and the Model Victorian Lady," in *Images of Victorian Womanhood in English Art* (London: Associated University Press, 1987), 87–96.

8 John Williamson Palmer, *Portfolio of Autograph Etchings* (Boston, 1881), 18.

9 Wentworth, 1978, 130.

10 *Architect*, May 19, 1877, 320.

11 Oscar Wilde, *Miscellanies* (London: Methuen, 1908), 20–21.

12 *Times*, May 1, 1877, 10.

13 *London Journal*, April 15, 1876, 252.

14 As an anonymous writer warned, "children's minds are like wax, readily receiving any impression" (*Children: Their Health, Training and Education* [London, 1879], 111).

15 Genesis 10:8–10. "And Cush beat Nimrod: he began to be a mighty one in the earth. He was a mighty hunter before the Lord." Tissot returned to the theme of Nimrod in his later illustrations for the New Testament, representing him as a man with a knife and deer carcasses.

The Seasons

1 He added with perhaps unnecessary honesty, "all this intimidated me so much that I never went to see him again" (Georgiana Burne-Jones, *Memorials of Edward Burne-Jones* [London: Macmillan, 1904], 281–82).

2 Palmer, 18. One fashion writer noted that at Tooth's Gallery, "J. J. Tissot is represented by several pictures in his favorite and justly popular style" (*Ladies' Gazette of Fashion* 1 [1879]: 146).

3 *World*, May 8, 1878, 9.

4 Baudelaire wrote, "if for the necessary and inevitable costume of an age you subsitute another, you will be guilty of a mistranslation" (in Mayne, 13).

5 As Anne Higonnet has remarked in her discussion of Berthe Morisot's attraction to the fashion plate, "what we call 'avant-garde art' has cyclically engaged, co-opted, transformed, and anesthetized popular imagery" (*Berthe Morisot's Images of Women* [Cambridge: Harvard University Press, 1992], 102). Higonnet cites Thomas Crow's "Modernism and Mass Culture in the Visual Arts," in *Modernism and Modernity: The Vancouver Conference Papers*, ed. Benjamin H. D. Buchloh, Serge Guilbaut, and David Solkin (Halifax: Press of the Nova Scotia College of Art and Design, 1983).

6 G. J. Whyte-Melville, *Roy's Wife* (London, 1878), 28.

7 Eliza Lynn Linton, "Costume and its Morals," *Saturday Review*, July 13, 1867, 144–45. Valerie Steele suggests that the fear of this caricature may have been a displaced anxiety about growing female independence (*Fashion and Eroticism: Ideals of Female Beauty from the Victorian Era to the Jazz Age* [Oxford: Oxford University Press, 1985], 130).

8 Roger Diederen, *European Paintings of the Nineteenth Century* (Cleveland: Cleveland Museum of Art, 1999).

9 George Halkett, *Notes to the Royal Manchester Institution* (London, 1878), 33.

10 Martin Hardie, *Frederick Goulding* (Stirling, 1914), 32.

11 Unpublished letter to John Williamson Palmer, December 2, 1881, Clifton Waller Barrett Library, #8099-A, Special Collections Department, University of Virginia Library.

12 Hardie, 35.

Declarations of Love

1 Wood, 120; Misfeldt, 1991, 126. Both remarks concern the etching *Summer Evening* (1881).

2 *Illustrated London News*, May 30, 1874, 511.

3 *Daily Telegraph*, May 10, 1879, 3.

4 *Spectator*, May 31, 1879, 691.

5 "A Brave Girl," *London Journal* (September 1876): 166.

6 "Househunting," September 22, 1883, 169, quoted in Donald J. Olsen, *The Growth of Victorian London* (New York: Penguin, 1976), 207.

7 *Illustrated London News*, May 3, 1879, 415.

8 Tom Carter, *The Victorian Garden* (London: Bell and Hyman, 1984), 67–88. See also Margaret Flanders Darby, "The Conservatory in St. John's Wood," in Lochnan.

9 The editor of the American portfolio in which the etching appeared claimed that the painting was done after the etching, which in turn was done for the portfolio in question (Palmer, 17).

10 Willard Misfeldt noted that Kathleen appears twice in the painting. *J. J. Tissot: Prints from the Gotlieb Collection*, 122.

11 Palmer, 17.

12 Ibid.

13 *Observer*, May 8, 1881, 6.

14 Baudelaire, "The Painter of Modern Life," in Mayne, 33–34.

15 *Standard*, April 30, 1881, 3.

16 Willard Misfeldt notes that the paintings *A Garden Bench* and *Little Nimrod* are the same size and format and were displayed together in Tissot's one-man show in the Palais de l'Industrie in 1883 (1991, 174).

17 John Farmer, *Twixt Two Worlds: A Narrative of the Life and Work of William Eglinton* (London, 1886), 187.

18 Jacques-Emile Blanche, *Portraits of a Lifetime*, trans. and ed. Walter Clement (London: Dent, 1937), 65–66.

19 Yveling Rambaud, "Force Psychique," *Revue Illustrée* 5 (1888): 39–47.

20 For more on Tissot and spiritualism, see Ann Saddlemyer, "Spirits in Space: Theatricality and the Occult in Tissot's Life and Art," and Serena Keshavjee, "Tissot and the Scientization of Spirituality," in Lochnan.

21 *Grammar of Painting and Engraving* (*Grammaire des Arts du Dessin*), trans. Kate Newell Doggett (New York, 1874), 281.

22 Edmond de Goncourt recorded the following visit to Tissot's house in Paris in the 1890s: "And in the dusk, refusing to look for candles, with a voice which he made mysterious and a vague gaze, he showed us a crystal bowl and an enamel plate, which served at his conjurings…He took up a convenient notebook, where he showed us entire pages containing the history of his conjurings, and he finally showed us a picture representing a woman with luminous hands, whom he said had come to embrace him and whom he had seen move her lips, her lips like lips of fire" (*Journal* 3:1118, in Wentworth, 1984, 178—my translation).

Parisiennes

1 Octave Uzanne, *Fashion in Paris*, trans. Lady Mary Lord (London, 1901), 1–2.

2 *L'Art Moderne*, May 10, 1885, 147.

3 *Builder*, May 22, 1886, 737.

4 Hardie, 82.

5 *Cassatt, A Retrospective*, ed. Nancy Moull Mathews (New York: Hugh Lauter Levin, 1996), 177.

6 See Tamar Garb, "James Tissot's 'Parisienne' and The Making of the Modern Woman," in *Bodies of Modernity: Figure and Flesh in Fin-de-Siècle France* (London: Thames and Hudson, 1998), 81–113.

7 See David Brooke, "James Tissot's *Amateur Circus*," *Boston Museum Bulletin* 67 (1969): 4–17.

8 For more about the French use of the word "to see" and the significance of the woman looker, see Deborah Bershad, "Looking, Power, and Sexuality: Degas' *Woman with a Lorgnette*," in Richard Kendall and Griselda Pollock, eds., *Dealing with Degas: Representations of Women and the Politics of Vision* (New York: Universe, 1991), 95–105, 99.

9 Garb, 1998, 100.

10 Ibid., 108.

11 C. Willett Cunnington quotes contemporary commentators in 1875 stating that the current fashion "is shameful and the female form is presented swathed in a thin and narrow covering which, while presenting its outlines almost as distinctly as those of an uncovered statue, has the property of burlesquing them" (*English Women's Clothing in the Nineteenth Century* [New York: Dover, 1990], 275–76).

12 Charles Blanc, *Art in Ornament and Dress* (New York, 1877), 273–74.

13 Misfeldt, 1991, 170.

14 Taxile Delord, *Physiologie de la Parisienne* (Paris, 1842), 21.

From Prodigal to Pilgrim

1 Gert Schiff, "Tissot's Illustrations for the Hebrew Bible," in *J. James Tissot: Biblical Paintings* (New York: The Jewish Museum, 1982), 23. The reproduction rights for the *Life of Christ* sold for one million francs, the exhibition entrance fees amounted to $100,000, and the Brooklyn Museum paid $60,000 for the watercolors (Wentworth, 1984, 187). In 1909 the Old Testament pictures were sold for $25,000–$30,000 to Jacob Schiff, who donated them to the New York Public Library (*New York Times*, February 6, 1909, in Tissot Scrapbook, New York Public Library); they were transferred to the Jewish Museum in 1952.

2 Wentworth, 1984, 172.

3 Unlabeled newsclipping, Tissot Scrapbook, New York Public Library.

4 *Bookman* (September–February 1905): 320.

5 *Churchman*, November 26, 1898, 780–2.

6 See Wentworth, 1984, 196, and Bernard Hanson, "D.W. Griffith: Some Sources," *Art Bulletin* 54 (December 1972): 493–515. Although the design of the ark was Tissot's, the watercolor in which it features was completed by a studio assistant after his death.

7 Ellen G. D'Oench, *Prodigal Son Narratives* (New Haven: Yale University Art Gallery, 1995), 10.

8 Unpublished letter to Charles Deschamps, no date, 1881, Special Collections, Getty Center Library.

9 Laver, 33.

10 Unpublished letter to John Williamson Palmer, December 2, 1881, Clifton Waller Barrett Library, #8099-A, Special Collections Department, University of Virginia Library.

11 D'Oench, 22. Tissot had painted a still life of shells in 1866 (Christie's, London, June 21, 1995) and probably had his own collection.

12 Christie's sale, New York, May 22, 1990.

13 Charles Eden, *Japan, Historical and Descriptive* (London, 1877), 180.

14 *Builder*, May 20, 1882, 606.

15 *Century Magazine*, 1898, Tissot Scrapbook, New York Public Library.

16 Unpublished letter to Mr. P. Cummings, Brookline (Brooklyn?), February 2, no year, Getty Center Library.

17 See Walter Cahn, "Solomonic Elements in Romanesque Art," in Joseph Gutmann, ed., *The Temple of Solomon: Archeological Fact and Medieval Tradition in Christian, Islamic, and Jewish Art* (Missoula, Montana: Scholars Press, 1976).

18 James Tissot, *The Life of Our Saviour Jesus Christ*, 4 vols. (New York, 1899), 1:15.

19 Ibid., 1:112.

20 *Collier's Weekly* 22, no. 13 (1899): 18.

21 Tissot, 1899, 2:203–5.

22 Ibid., 206.

23 Personal communication, December 1998.

24 Tissot, 1899, 3:53–54.

25 Ibid., 1:53.

26 Ibid., 4:190.

27 Ibid., 1:52.

28 Ibid., 1:ix.

29 Ibid., 4:271.

30 I am very grateful for the scholarly knowledge and opinions of Harold Attridge, Margot Fassler, and Jaime Lara, who identified and interpreted the religious objects.

31 Tissot, 1899, 1:26–27.

32 *New York Times Magazine*, December 11, 1898, 7.

33 Pierpont Morgan purchased an edition at this price. *Chicago Inter-Ocean*, August 6, 1905, no page number in Chicago Art Institute Scrapbooks, 21:60.

34 Unpublished letter to McClure, Paris, April 21, 1899. Getty Center Library.

35 Ibid.

36 Thanks to Willard Misfeldt for calling these photographs to my attention.

37 Schiff, 40.

38 Michael Booth, *Victorian Spectacular Theatre* (Boston: Routledge and Kegan Paul, 1981), 174.

Chronology

Most of this information has been drawn from Brooke, 1968; Misfeldt, 1971; Jewish Museum, 1982; and Wentworth, 1984 (see *Bibliography*).

1836   Jacques-Joseph Tissot born in Nantes to Marcel-Théodore Tissot, a linen-draper and merchant and Marie Durand, a milliner. Family moves to Château de Buillon, near Besançon, which Tissot inherited and retired to at the end of his life.

c. 1848   Enrolls in Jesuit schools in Flanders, Brittany and the Jura.

c. 1856   Leaves Nantes to settle in Paris; meets Whistler, changes name to James.

1857   Registers to copy paintings at the Louvre.

c. 1858   Becomes friendly with Degas. Studies with academic painters Louis Lamothe and Hippolyte Flandrin.

1859   Debut at Paris Salon, five paintings. Visit to Antwerp, admiring work of Hendrik Leys.

1861   Six paintings at Salon.

1862   Travels to Florence and Venice.

1863   Three paintings at Salon. Becomes close friend of Alphonse Daudet, novelist.

1864   One painting at Royal Academy exhibition and two at Society of British Artists, London. Probable trip to London. Two paintings at Salon. Begins to become renowned collector of Japanese art.

1865   Two paintings at Salon.

1866   Two paintings at Salon; wins medal, placing him *hors concours*.

1867   Sets up house at 64 avenue de l'Impératrice (later avenue du Bois de Boulogne). Two works at Salon. Becomes drawing teacher of Japanese Prince.

1867–73   Exhibits in London, French Gallery.

1868   One painting, one pastel, one watercolor at Salon.

1869   Possible visit to London. First caricatures for Thomas Gibson Bowles's magazine *Vanity Fair*. Two paintings at Salon.

1870   Two paintings at Salon. Franco-Prussian War: Joins company of sharpshooters, the *Eclaireurs de la Seine* (later the *Tirailleurs de la Seine*), part of the *Garde National* during Franco-Prussian War. Lives in Paris with Thomas Gibson Bowles. Completes drawings of the war for Bowles's book *The Defence of Paris, Narrated As It Was Seen*, 1871.

1871   Possible involvement in Paris Commune. June: moves to London.

1872   Two paintings at Royal Academy (R.A.).

1873   Purchases home in St. John's Wood. Three paintings at R.A.

1874   Three paintings at R.A. Return trip to Paris. Berthe Morisot visits him in London. Travels to Venice with Manet and purchases (or is given) the latter's painting *Blue Venice*.

1875   Two paintings at R.A.

c. 1876   Begins living with Kathleen Newton.

1876   Three paintings and one etching at R.A. Two etchings at Salon. First ten etchings issued in volume form. Seven works in *Premier exposition des ouvrages executés en noir et blanc*, Galerie Durand-Ruel, Paris.

1877   Ten works at Grosvenor Gallery; stops exhibiting at Royal Academy until 1881.

1878–82   Exhibits widely in Britain: at Brighton Art Gallery; Art Association, Newcastle; Walker Art Gallery, Liverpool; Royal Manchester Institution; Manchester Exhibition of Works in Black and

White; Art Treasures Exhibition, Wrexham; Yorkshire Fine Arts Society, Leeds; Glasgow Institute of Fine Arts; City Art Gallery, Glasgow; Exhibition of Works in Black and White, Glasgow; Royal Society of Artists, Birmingham; Dudley Gallery, London; Goupil Gallery, London; Thomas Maclean's Gallery, London; Arthur Tooth Gallery, London; New Continental Gallery, London.

1881   Two paintings at R.A. Also exhibits with Society of Painter-Etchers.

1882   May: One-man exhibition at Dudley Gallery, London, "J. J. Tissot: An Exhibition of Modern Art." Trip to Paris to discuss illustrations for Edmond de Goncourt's *Renée Mauperin*. Death of Kathleen Newton, November 9. Permanent return to France shortly after Newton's death.

1883   One-man exhibition in Paris, Palais de l'Industrie. Exhibits with Société d'aquarellistes français.

c. 1883   Engagement to Louise Riesener, daughter of painter Louis Riesener, broken by her around 1885.

1884   Exhibits with Société d'aquarellistes français.

1884–86   Maintains foothold in English market with exhibitions at Hanover Gallery, London.

1885   Works with English medium William Eglinton and holds séances. May 20: records image of successful contact with spirit of Kathleen Newton. Exhibits series of *La Femme à Paris* at Galerie Sedelmeyer, Paris.

1886   *La Femme à Paris* (entitled *Pictures of Parisian Life*), with etchings, exhibited at Arthur Tooth Gallery, London. Exhibits with Société d'aquarellistes français. October: Leaves for Middle East to begin illustrations for *Life of Christ*.

1887   March: returns to Paris. Contributes to *Exposition de gravures du siècle*, Galerie Georges Petit, Paris.

1888   Exhibits three works in International Exhibition, Glasgow.

1889   Exhibits at Paris Exposition Universelle, wins gold medal for Prodigal Son series. Contributes to *Exposition de Peintres-Graveurs*, at Galerie Durand-Ruel, Paris. Second Trip to Middle East.

1894   Exhibits first illustrations of the *Life of Christ* in Paris at Salon of the Société Nationale des Beaux-Arts, Paris.

1895   Exhibits complete series of 365 illustrations for *Life of Christ* in Paris.

1896   Complete *Life of Christ* series shown in London. *La Vie de Notre Seigneur Jésus-Christ* published in France. Third trip to Palestine to start on Old Testament Illustrations.

1897   *The Life of Our Saviour Jesus Christ* published in London and New York. Visits U.S. in two separate trips to promote tour of *Life of Christ* watercolors.

1898–99   New Testament watercolors tour New York, Chicago, St. Louis, Omaha, and other cities.

1900   New Testament watercolors acquired by public subscription by Brooklyn Museum.

1901   95 of the Old Testament illustrations appear at Salon of the Société Nationale des Beaux-Arts, Paris.

1902   August 8, Tissot dies, leaving Old Testament project uncompleted. Series finished by assistants, partially after Tissot's own designs.

1903   Complete set of Old Testament watercolors appears in Paris.

1904   *Holy Bible: The Old Testament* published in Paris, London, and New York.

1904–8   Old Testament watercolors, including works by other artists, tour the United States: New York, Chicago, Detroit, and other cities. Acquired by private collector who donates them to the New York Public Library (later transferred to the Jewish Museum).

Bibliography

Abdy, Jane. *J. J. Tissot: Etchings, Drypoints and Mezzotints.* London: Lumley Cazalet Gallery, 1978.

Amaya, M. "Painter of 'la Mystérieuse.'" *Apollo* (August 1962): 472–74.

d'Argencourt, Louise, and Douglas Druick. *The Other Nineteenth Century: Paintings and Sculptures in the Collection of Mrs. and Mrs. Joseph Tannenbaum.* Ottawa: National Gallery of Canada, 1978.

Ash, Russell. *James Tissot.* New York: Abrams, 1992.

Bastard, Georges. "James Tissot: Notes Intimes." *Revue de Bretagne* 36 (November 1906): 253–78.

Béraldi, Henri. *Les Graveurs du XIXème siècle.* Tome 12. Paris, 1885–92. 125–34.

Blanche, Jacques-Emile. *Portraits of a Lifetime.* Translated and edited by Walter Clement. London: Dent, 1936.

——. *More Portraits of a Lifetime.* Translated and edited by Walter Clement. London: Dent, 1939.

Bowles, Thomas Gibson. *The Defence of Paris Narrated As It Was Seen.* London, 1871. Illustrated by Tissot.

——. *Flotsam and Jetsam.* London, 1882.

Brooke, David S. "James Tissot and the 'ravissante Irlandaise.'" *Connoisseur* (May 1968): 55–59.

——. "Tissot's *The Parting.*" *Amgueddfa: Bulletin of the National Museum of Wales* (Summer–Autumn 1969): 22–26.

——. "James Tissot's *Amateur Circus.*" *Boston Museum Bulletin* 67 (1969): 4–17.

——. "An Interesting Story by James Tissot." *Art Bulletin of Victoria* (1969–1970): 22–29.

Brooke, David S., Michael Wentworth, and Henri Zerner. *James Jacques Joseph Tissot, 1836–1902: A Retrospective Exhibition.* Providence: Museum of Art, Rhode Island School of Design, 1968.

Bryan's Dictionary of Painters and Engravers. London, 1905.

Burroughs, Louise. "A Portrait of James Tissot by Degas." *Bulletin of the Metropolitan Museum of Art* 36 (February 1941): 35–38.

Carr, J. Comyns. *Coasting Bohemia.* London: Macmillan, 1914.

Chugi, Ikagama. "Tissot: Drawing Instructor of Tokugawa Akitake." In *Japonisme in Art: An International Symposium.* Edited by Chisaburo Yamada et al. New York, 1981.

Claretie, Jules. "M. James Tissot." *Peintres et sculpteurs contemporains.* Paris, 1873.

Degas, Edgar. *Degas Letters.* Edited by Marcel Guérin and translated by Marguerite Kay. Oxford: Cassirer, 1948.

Denvir, B. "Ingenious Explorer." *Art and Artists* 13 (May 1978): 32–35.

Dudley Gallery. *An Exhibition of Modern Art by J. J. Tissot.* London, 1882.

Farmer, John S. *"Twixt Two Worlds": A Narrative of the Life and Work of William Eglinton.* London, 1886.

Galinou, Mireille. "Greenfinger Painting." *Country Life* (July 13, 1989): 120–23.

Goncourt, Edmond and Jules de. *Renée Mauperin: édition ornée de dix compositions à l'eau-forte par James Tissot.* Charpentier, 1884.

——. *Journal: mémories de la vie littéraire.* Paris: Flammarion, 1956.

Gourley III, Hugh J. "Tissots in the Museum's Collection." *Bulletin of the Rhode Island School of Design* (March 1964): 1–4.

Graves Art Gallery, Sheffield. *Paintings, Drawings and Etchings by James Tissot.* London: The Arts Council, 1955.

Hughes, J. H. "Tissot's Contribution to Religious Art." *Brush and Pencil* 10 (1902): 357–68.

James, Henry. "The Picture Season in London, 1877," *Galaxy* (August 1877), reprinted in *The Painter's Eye: Notes and Essays on the Pictorial Arts by Henry James.* Edited by John L. Sweeney. Cambridge: Harvard University Press, 1956.

Janis, Eugenia Parry. "Tissot Retrospective." *The Burlington Magazine* 110 (May 1968): 300–3.

Jewish Museum. *J. James Tissot: Biblical Paintings.* With essays by Yochanan Muffs and Gert Schiff and a chronology by Michael Wentworth and David S. Brooke. New York: The Jewish Museum, 1982.

Jopling, Louise. *Twenty Years of My Life.* London: John Lane, 1925.

Knoblock, E. "James Tissot and the Seventies." *Apollo* 17 (June 1933): 255–58.

——. "The Whimsical Seventies." *Country Life* 80 (December 26, 1936): 678–79.

Knoedler, Edmond. *Modern Etchers.* New York, 1891

Knoedler, M. & Co., New York. *A Painter Etcher: The Etched Work of J. J. Tissot.* (1886–87).

Laver, James. *"Vulgar Society": The Romantic Career of James Tissot.* London: Constable, 1936.

Leicester Galleries. *In the Seventies: Catalogue of an Exhibition of Paintings by James Tissot.* London, 1933.

——. *Catalogue of the Second James Tissot Exhibition.* London, 1937.

Levy, Clifton Harby. "J. James Tissot and his Work." *New Outlook* 60 (1898): 954–64.

Lochnan, Katharine, ed. *Seductive Surfaces: The Art of Tissot.* Studies in British Art 6. New Haven and London: Yale University Press, 1999.

Lostalot, Alfred de. "James Tissot." *Société d'aquarellistes français, ouvrages d'art.* Tome 2. Paris, 1883.

——. "Le Musée des Arts Décoratifs: exposition de MM. Le Comte Lepic et James Tissot." *Gazette des Beaux-Arts,* 2nd pér., 27 (1883): 445–56.

Macdonald, Margaret, and Joy Newton. "Letters from the Whistler Collection." *Gazette des Beaux-Arts* (December 1986): 201–14.

Marshall, Nancy Rose. "'Transcripts of Modern Life:' The London Paintings of James Tissot, 1871–1882," Ph.D. diss., Yale University, 1998.

Matyjaszkiewicz, Krystyna, ed. *James Tissot.* London: Phaidon Press and Barbican Art Gallery, 1984.

Misfeldt, Willard. "The Hermit of Buillon: A James Tissot Legend." College Art Association of America, Papers, 1971.

——. "James Jacques Joseph Tissot: A Bio-Critical Study." Ph.D. diss., Washington University. Ann Arbor, Michigan: University Microfilms International, 1971.

——. *The Albums of James Tissot.* Bowling Green, Ohio: Bowling Green University Popular Press, 1982.

——. "James Tissot's Abbaye de Buillon." *Apollo* (January 1984): 24–29.

——. "James Tissot and Alphonse Daudet: Friends and Collaborators." *Apollo* (February 1986): 110–15.

——. *J. J. Tissot. Prints from the Gotlieb Collection.* Alexandria, Virginia: Arts International, 1991.

Moffett, Cleveland. "J. J. Tissot and his Paintings of the Life of Christ." *McClure's Magazine* 12 (March 1899): 386–96.

Monkhouse, Cosmo. *British Contemporary Artists.* New York, 1899.

Montesquiou-Fézensac, Robert comte de. "Tissot Chrétien." *Revue illustrée* (1896): 324–32.

Morisot, Berthe. *Correspondence.* Edited by Denis Rouart and translated by Betty W. Hubbard. London: Camden Town Press, 1986.

Musée des Beaux-Arts de Besançon. *James Tissot, 1836–1902.* Besançon: Musée des Beaux-Arts, 1985.

Palmer, John Williamson. *Portfolio of Autograph Etchings* Boston, 1881.

Preston, Harley. "Tissot and *Renée Mauperin*." *Apollo* (June 1994): 442–44.

Rambaud, Yveling. "Force Psychique." *Revue illustrée* (1888): 39–47.

Roditi, Edouard. "Tissot: Revolutionary, Dandy, Realist." *Arts* 42 (May 1968): 44–46.

Ross, Marita. "The Truth About Tissot." *Everybody's Weekly* (June 15, 1946): 6–7.

——. "Un Mystère de l'époque victorienne." *Bulletin de la Société Archéologique et Historique de Nantes et de Loire-Inférieure* (1947): 88–93.

Rutter, Frank. "Tissot Exhibition." *Connoisseur* (June 1933): 91.

"Second Tissot Exhibition at the Leicester Gallery, The." *Apollo* 25 (February 1937): 110.

Sedelmeyer, Galerie . *Exposition J.-J. Tissot: quinze tableaux sur la Femme à Paris.* Paris, 1885.

Sertillanges, A. D. "L'Œuvre de James Tissot et 'l'Edition Mame.'" *Correspondant* 24 (1896): II.

Sherard, R. H. "James Tissot and his Life of Christ." *Magazine of Art* 18 (1895): 1–8.

Strahan, Edward. "Tissot and the 'Medievalists.'" In *Modern French Art.* New York, 1882.

Storey, G. A. *Sketches from Memory.* London, 1899.

Taylor, Tom. *Ballads and Songs of Brittany.* London, 1865. Illustrated by Tissot.

Thiebault-Sisson, François. "J. James Tissot." *Les Arts* 9 (August 1902): 6.

Thomson, Ian. "Tissot and Oxford." *Oxford Art Journal* 2 (April 1979): 53–57.

——. "Tissot's Enigmatic Signatures." *Gazette des Beaux-Arts* (May–June 1985): 223–24.

Tissot, James. *Ten Etchings.* London, 1876.

——. *Eaux-Fortes, manière noire, pointes sèches.* Paris, 1886.

——. *La Vie de Notre Seigneur Jésus-Christ.* 2 vols. Tours: Mame et fils, 1896–97.

——. *The Life of Our Saviour Jesus Christ.* 4 vols. Translated by Mrs. Arthur Bell. London, 1897.

——. *The Life of Our Saviour Jesus Christ.* 4 vols. New York, 1899.

——. *Holy Bible: The Old Testament: Three Hundred and Ninety-Six Compositions Illustrating the Old Testament.* Paris, London, New York, 1904.

"Tissot: The Shrewd Observer." *Apollo* 87 (June 1968): 464.

Tooth, Arthur, and Sons. *Pictures of Parisian Life by J. J. Tissot.* London, 1886.

"Town Garden, A." *Country Life* (November 23, 1912): 716–18.

Union Centrale des Arts Décoratifs. *Exposition des œuvres de M. J.-J. Tissot.* Paris, 1883.

"'Victorian Life' Exhibition at the Leicester Galleries, The." *Apollo* 26 (August 1937): 107–8.

Warner, Malcolm. *Tissot.* London: Medici Society, 1982.

Waters, Clara Erskine Clement and Lawrence Hutton. *Artists of the Nineteenth Century.* Boston and New York, 1879.

Wentworth, Michael. "James Tissot—A Retrospective View." *Canadian Antiques Collector* 3 (April 1968): 10–13.

——. "Tissot's *On the Thames, A Heron.*" *Minneapolis Institute of Arts Bulletin* 62 (1975): 35–49.

——. *James Tissot: Catalogue Raisonné of his Prints.* Minneapolis: Minneapolis Institute of Arts, and Williamstown, Massachusetts: Sterling and Francine Clark Art Institute, 1978.

——. "Energized Punctuality: James Tissot's *Gentleman in a Railway Carriage.*" *Worcester Art Museum Journal* (1979–1980): 9–27.

——. "Tissot and Japonisme." In *Japonisme in Art: An International Symposium.* Edited by Chisaburo Yamada et. al. New York, 1981.

——. *James Tissot.* Oxford: Clarendon Press, 1984.

Wood, Christopher. *Tissot: The Life and Work of Jacques Joseph Tissot, 1836–1902.* Boston: Little, Brown, 1986.

Zerner, Henri. "The Return of 'James' Tissot." *Artnews* 67 (March 1968): 32–35; 68–69.

——. "James Tissot." *L'Œil* 160 (April 1968): 22–29.

Authors' Acknowledgments

For their various kindnesses during the preparation of the exhibition and the writing of the catalogue, the authors would like to thank the following: Lady Abdy, Carol Armstrong, Richard Reed Armstrong, Caroline Arscott, Martin Beisly, Martin Berger, Elspeth Brown, Tom Crow, Bernard Derroitte, Benjamin Doller, John House, Andrew Kalman, Nicholas Maclean, Olivier Meslay, Esther Da Costa Meyer, Gabriel Naughton, Claire O'Mahony, Carolyn Peter, Jules D. Prown, Britt Salvesen, Polly Sartori, Simon Taylor, Roxana Velásquez, and Michael Wentworth.

The American Federation of Arts